CUANTUM

PYTHON
PROGRAMMING
UNLOCKED FOR BEGINNERS

UPDATED 2023

Python Programming Unlocked for Beginners

First Edition

Copyright © 2023 Cuantum Technologies

All rights reserved. No part of this book may be reproduced, stored in a retrieval system, or transmitted in any form or by any means, without the prior written permission of the publisher, except in the case of brief quotations embedded in critical articles or reviews. Every effort has been made in the preparation of this book to ensure the accuracy of the information presented.

However, the information contained in this book is sold without warranty, either express or implied. Neither the author, nor Cuantum Technologies or its dealers and distributors, will be held liable for any damages caused or alleged to have been caused directly or indirectly by this book.

Cuantum Technologies has endeavored to provide trademark information about all of the companies and products mentioned in this book by the appropriate use of capitals. However, Cuantum Technologies cannot guarantee the accuracy of this information.

First edition: April 2023

Published by Cuantum Technologies LLC.

Dallas, TX.

ISBN 9798389919716

"Learning to write programs stretches your mind, and helps you think better, creates a way of thinking about things that I think is helpful in all domains."

- Bill Gates

CLAIM YOUR
FREE MONTH

As part of our reward program for our readers, we want to give you a **full free month** of...

CUANTUM AI
www.cuantum.ai

THE PROCESS IS SIMPLE

1 Go to Amazon and leave us your amazing book review

2 Send us your name and date of review to books@cuantum.tech

3 Join **cuantum.ai** and we will activate the Creator Plan for you, free of charge.

What is CuantumAI?

All-in-one AI powered content generator and money factory

A complete Eco-system

AI Powerded Chatbot Mentors - Templates - Documents - Images - Audio/Text Transcriptions - And more...

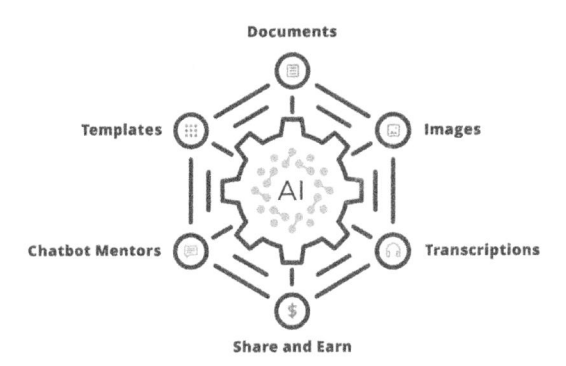

- Documents
- Templates
- Images
- Chatbot Mentors
- Transcriptions
- Share and Earn

Get all your AI needs in one place to boost productivity, advance your career, or start an AI-powered business.

Do the research - Write the content - Generate the Image - Publish - Earn Money

CLAIM IT TODAY! LIMITED AVAILABILITY

TABLE OF CONTENTS

TABLE OF CONTENTS 5
WHO WE ARE 14
    Our Philosophy: 15
    Our Expertise: 15
INTRODUCTION 16
CHAPTER 1: INTRODUCTION TO PYTHON 19
1.1 PYTHON: A VERSATILE AND BEGINNER-FRIENDLY PROGRAMMING LANGUAGE 19
    1.2 A little bit of Python's History and Guido van Rossum's Role in its Development 20
    1.3 Differences between Python 2.x and Python 3.x 21
1.4 INSTALLING PYTHON AND SETTING UP A DEVELOPMENT ENVIRONMENT 24
    1.4.1 Installing Python 24
    1.4.2 Setting Up a Development Environment 28
CHAPTER 2: PYTHON BASICS 44
2.1 PYTHON SYNTAX 44
    2.1.1 Indentation 44
    2.1.2 Comments 45
    2.1.3 Variables 45
    2.1.4 Statements and Expressions 46
    2.1.5 Basic Data Types and Operators 47
    Exercise 2.1.1: Calculate the Area of a Rectangle 48
    Exercise 2.1.2: Printing a Triangle 49
    Exercise 2.1.3: Printing a Multiplication Table 50
2.2 VARIABLES AND DATA TYPES 52
    2.2.1 Variables 52
    2.2.2 Data Types 53
    2.2.3 Type Conversion 53
    Exercise 2.2.1: Celsius to Fahrenheit Converter 54

EXERCISE 2.2.2: CALCULATE THE AREA AND PERIMETER OF A RECTANGLE 55
EXERCISE 2.2.3: SIMPLE INTEREST CALCULATOR 56

2.3 OPERATORS 58

2.3.1 ARITHMETIC OPERATORS 58
2.3.2 COMPARISON OPERATORS 59
2.3.4 LOGICAL OPERATOR 60
2.3.5 BITWISE OPERATORS 61
EXERCISE 2.3.1: SIMPLE ARITHMETIC OPERATIONS 61
EXERCISE 2.3.2: MAXIMUM OF TWO NUMBERS 63
EXERCISE 2.3.3: CALCULATE THE DISTANCE BETWEEN TWO POINTS 64

2.4 TYPE CONVERSION 65

2.4.1 BASIC TYPE CONVERSION FUNCTIONS 65
2.4.2 TYPE CONVERSION LIMITATIONS 66
2.4.3 IMPLICIT TYPE CONVERSION 66
EXERCISE 2.4.1: SHOPPING LIST PRICE CALCULATOR 67
EXERCISE 2.4.2: CALCULATE THE AVERAGE OF THREE NUMBERS 68
EXERCISE 2.4.3: CONVERT SECONDS TO HOURS, MINUTES, AND SECONDS 69

2.5 INPUT AND OUTPUT 70

2.5.1 OUTPUT: THE print() FUNCTION 70
2.5.2 INPUT: THE input() FUNCTION 71
2.5.3 FORMATTING OUTPUT: F-STRINGS, STR.FORMAT(), AND %-FORMATTING 72
EXERCISE 2.5.1: PERSONALIZED GREETING 74
EXERCISE 2.5.2: PERSONAL INFORMATION FORM 75
EXERCISE 2.5.3: CALCULATE THE AREA AND CIRCUMFERENCE OF A CIRCLE 76

CHAPTER 3: DATA STRUCTURES 78

3.1: LISTS 78

EXERCISE 3.1.1: CREATING AND ACCESSING LISTS 81
EXERCISE 3.1.2: LIST MANIPULATION 81
EXERCISE 3.1.3: LIST SLICING 82

3.2: TUPLES 83

3.2.1: CREATING TUPLES: 83
3.2.2: ACCESSING TUPLE ELEMENTS: 84
3.2.3: TUPLE UNPACKING: 85
3.2.4: IMMUTABILITY: 85
EXERCISE 3.2.1: CREATING TUPLES 86
EXERCISE 3.2.2: ACCESSING TUPLE ELEMENTS 87
EXERCISE 3.2.3: TUPLE UNPACKING 88

3.3: SETS 89

3.3.1: Creating a Set: 89
3.3.2: Adding and Removing Elements: 90
3.3.3: Set Operations: 91
Exercise 3.3.1: Creating and Modifying Sets 92
Exercise 3.3.2: Set Operations 93
Exercise 3.3.3: Set Comprehension 94

3.4: DICTIONARIES 95

Exercise 3.4.1: Create a Dictionary 98
Exercise 3.4.2: Accessing and Modifying Dictionary Values 99
Exercise 3.4.3: Iterating Over a Dictionary 100

CHAPTER 4: CONTROL STRUCTURES 102

4.1: CONDITIONAL STATEMENTS (IF, ELIF, ELSE) 102

Exercise 4.1.1: Odd or Even Number 105
Exercise 4.1.2: Age Group Classification 106
Exercise 4.1.3: Letter Grade Calculation 107

4.2: LOOPS (FOR, WHILE) 109

4.2.1 for Loop: 109
4.2.2 range() Function: 110
4.2.3 while Loop: 111
Exercise 4.2.1: Sum of Numbers 113
Exercise 4.2.2: Reverse a String 114
Exercise 4.2.3: Countdown Timer 115

4.3: LOOP CONTROL (BREAK, CONTINUE) 116

4.3.1 break Statement: 116
4.3.2 continue Statement: 117
Exercise 4.3.1: Print First Five Even Numbers 119
Exercise 4.3.2: Sum of Positive Numbers 120
Exercise 4.3.3: Find the First Factor 121

4.4: NESTED CONTROL STRUCTURES 122

4.4.1: Nested Conditional Statements: 122
4.4.2: Nested Loops: 123
Exercise 4.4.1: Grade Calculator 124
Exercise 4.4.2: Multiplication Table 125
Exercise 4.4.3: Triangle Pattern 126

CHAPTER 5: FUNCTIONS 128

5.1: DEFINING FUNCTIONS 128
- EXERCISE 5.1.1: SIMPLE GREETING FUNCTION 130
- EXERCISE 5.1.2: SUM OF TWO NUMBERS 131
- EXERCISE 5.1.3: AREA OF A RECTANGLE 132

5.2: FUNCTION ARGUMENTS 133
- 5.2.1: POSITIONAL ARGUMENTS: 133
- 5.2.2: KEYWORD ARGUMENTS: 134
- 5.2.3: DEFAULT ARGUMENTS: 135
- 5.2.4: VARIABLE-LENGTH ARGUMENTS: 136
- EXERCISE 5.2.1: SIMPLE CALCULATOR 138
- EXERCISE 5.2.2: GREETING WITH DEFAULT ARGUMENT 139
- EXERCISE 5.2.3: SUM OF NUMBERS WITH VARIABLE-LENGTH ARGUMENTS 140

5.3: RETURN VALUES 141
- EXAMPLE 1: SIMPLE ADDITION FUNCTION 142
- EXAMPLE 2: MAXIMUM OF TWO NUMBERS 142
- EXAMPLE 3: RETURN MULTIPLE VALUES 143
- EXERCISE 5.3.1: CALCULATE AREA OF A RECTANGLE 143
- EXERCISE 5.3.2: CHECK IF A NUMBER IS EVEN OR ODD 144
- EXERCISE 5.3.3: GET THE LENGTH OF A STRING 145

5.4: SCOPE OF VARIABLES 145
- 5.4.1: GLOBAL SCOPE: 145
- 5.4.2: LOCAL SCOPE: 146
- EXERCISE 5.4.1: ACCESSING GLOBAL VARIABLES INSIDE A FUNCTION 148
- EXERCISE 5.4.2: MODIFYING GLOBAL VARIABLES INSIDE A FUNCTION 148
- EXERCISE 5.4.3: LOCAL VARIABLES VS. GLOBAL VARIABLES 149

5.5: LAMBDA FUNCTIONS 150
- EXERCISE 5.5.1: LAMBDA SQUARE 152
- EXERCISE 5.5.2: LAMBDA LIST SORTING 153
- EXERCISE 5.5.3: LAMBDA WITH FILTER 153

CHAPTER 6: WORKING WITH FILES 155

6.1: OPENING AND CLOSING FILES 155
- EXERCISE 6.1.1: CREATE A NEW FILE 158
- EXERCISE 6.1.2: READ A FILE 158
- EXERCISE 6.1.3: APPEND TO A FILE 159

6.2: READING AND WRITING FILES 161

6.2.2: Writing multiple lines to a file: 161
6.2.3: Reading and writing binary files: 162
Exercise 6.2.1: Counting Lines in a Text File 163
Exercise 6.2.2: Reversing Lines in a Text File 163
Exercise 6.2.3: Read and Write a Binary File 164

6.3: File Modes and Operations 165

Exercise 6.3.1: Counting Lines in a File 167
Exercise 6.3.2: Copying a File 169
Exercise 6.3.3: Reading a Specific Line 170

6.4: Handling Exceptions in File Operations 171

Exercise 6.4.1: Handling FileNotFoundError 173
Exercise 6.4.2: Handling PermissionError 174
Exercise 6.4.3: Using Finally Block 175

Chapter 7: Modules and Packages 177

7.1: Importing Modules 177

Exercise 7.1.1: Random Number Generator 179
Exercise 7.1.2: Current Date and Time 180
Exercise 7.1.3: Calculate the Area of a Circle 181

7.2: Standard Library Modules 182

7.2.1: os 182
7.2.2: sys 183
7.2.3: re 183
7.2.4: json 184
7.2.5: urllib 184
Exercise 7.2.1: Create a Simple Module 186
Exercise 7.2.2: Create a Custom Text Manipulation Module 187
Exercise 7.2.3: Create a Module with Constants 189

7.3: Creating Your Own Modules 191

7.3.1: To create a Python package, follow these steps: 191
Exercise 7.3.1: Creating a Simple Math Package 194
Exercise 7.3.2: Creating a Text Processing Package 196
Exercise 7.3.3: Creating a Geometry Package 197

7.4 Python Packages 198

7.4.1: Creating a package: 199
7.4.2: Adding modules to a package: 199
7.4.3: Importing and using packages: 199

EXERCISE 7.4.1: CREATING AND USING A SIMPLE PACKAGE 201
EXERCISE 7.4.2: CREATING A PACKAGE 203
EXERCISE 7.4.3: USING THIRD-PARTY PACKAGES 205

CHAPTER 8: OBJECT-ORIENTED PROGRAMMING 207

8.1 CLASSES AND OBJECTS 207

EXERCISE 8.1.1: DEFINE A CAR CLASS 210
EXERCISE 8.1.2: DEFINE A CIRCLE CLASS 210
EXERCISE 8.1.3: DEFINE A BANKACCOUNT CLASS 211

8.2: ATTRIBUTES AND METHODS 212

8.2.1: ATTRIBUTES: 213
8.2.2: METHODS: 214
EXERCISE 8.2.1: CAR ATTRIBUTES AND METHODS 216
EXERCISE 8.2.2: BANK ACCOUNT 217
EXERCISE 8.2.3: CIRCLE CLASS 218

8.3: INHERITANCE 219

EXERCISE 8.3.1: SIMPLE INHERITANCE 222
EXERCISE 8.3.2: INHERITANCE AND METHOD OVERRIDING 223
EXERCISE 8.3.3: MULTIPLE INHERITANCE 224

8.4: POLYMORPHISM 225

8.4.1: METHOD OVERLOADING: 225
8.4.2: METHOD OVERRIDING: 225
8.4.3: DUCK TYPING: 226
EXERCISE 8.4.1: METHOD OVERLOADING 228
EXERCISE 8.4.2: METHOD OVERRIDING 229
EXERCISE 8.4.3: DUCK TYPING 230

8.5: ENCAPSULATION 231

8.5.1: PUBLIC MEMBERS: 231
8.5.2: PROTECTED MEMBERS: 231
8.5.3: PRIVATE MEMBERS: 232
EXERCISE 8.5.1: CREATE A SIMPLE EMPLOYEE CLASS 234
EXERCISE 8.5.2: IMPLEMENTING A CIRCLE CLASS 235
EXERCISE 8.5.3: CREATING A PASSWORD PROTECTED ACCOUNT 236

CHAPTER 9: ERROR HANDLING AND EXCEPTIONS 238

9.1 COMMON PYTHON ERRORS 238

9.1.1: SYNTAX ERRORS: 239

9.1.2: Exceptions: 239
    Exercise 9.1.1: Identify Syntax Errors 240
    Exercise 9.1.2: Identify Exception Errors 242
    Exercise 9.1.3: Raise Custom Exception 243

9.2: HANDLING EXCEPTIONS WITH TRY AND EXCEPT 244
    Exercise 9.2.1: Safe File Reading 247
    Exercise 9.2.2: Safe Division 248
    Exercise 9.2.3: Safe List Indexing 249

9.3: RAISING EXCEPTIONS 250
    Exercise 9.3.1: Raising Exceptions for Invalid Input 251
    Exercise 9.3.2: Raising Exceptions for Invalid Passwords 252
    Exercise 9.3.3: Raising Exceptions for Invalid Email Addresses 254

9.4: CUSTOM EXCEPTIONS 255
    Exercise 9.4.1: Create a custom exception for negative numbers 257
    Exercise 9.4.2: Create a custom exception for empty input strings 258
    Exercise 9.4.3: Create a custom exception for invalid usernames 260

CHAPTER 10: PYTHON BEST PRACTICES 262

10.1 PEP 8 - STYLE GUIDE FOR PYTHON CODE 262
    10.1.1: Indentation: 262
    10.1.2: Maximum Line Length: 263
    10.1.3: Imports: 264
    10.1.4: Whitespace: 265
    10.1.5: Naming Conventions: 265
    10.1.6: Comments: 266
    10.1.7: Docstrings: 267
    Exercise 10.1.1: PEP 8 Indentation 269
    Exercise 10.1.2: PEP 8 Imports 269
    Exercise 10.1.3: PEP 8 Naming Conventions 270

10.2: CODE COMMENTING AND DOCUMENTATION 271
    10.2.1: Inline comments: 272
    10.2.2: Block comments: 272
    10.2.3: Docstrings: 273
    Exercise 10.2.1: Inline Commenting 274
    Exercise 10.2.2: Block Commenting 275
    Exercise 10.2.3: Writing Docstrings 277

10.3: NAMING CONVENTIONS 278

    10.3.1: Variables and functions: 278
    10.3.2: Constants: 278
    10.3.3: Classes: 279
    10.3.4: Modules: 279
    10.3.5: Private variables and methods: 279
    Exercise 10.3.1: Identifying Incorrect Naming Conventions 280
    Exercise 10.3.2: Applying Naming Conventions 281
    Exercise 10.3.3: Refactoring Code with Proper Naming Conventions 282

10.4: CODE REUSABILITY AND MODULARIZATION 284

    10.4.1: Code Reusability: 284
    10.4.2: Modularization: 284
    10.4.3: Best Practices: 285
    10.4.4: Code Reusability Examples: 285
    Exercise 10.4.1: Reusable function for Fibonacci series 288
    Exercise 10.4.2: Create a reusable module for string manipulation 289
    Exercise 10.4.3: Organize a package for geometry calculations 290

CHAPTER 11: PROJECT: BUILD A SIMPLE APPLICATION 293

11.1: PLANNING YOUR PROJECT 293

    11.1.1: TaskMaster Application 294

11.2: IMPLEMENTING THE TASKMASTER PROJECT 295

11.3: TESTING AND DEBUGGING THE TASKMASTER PROJECT 297

    11.3.1: Unit testing: 297
    11.3.2: Integration testing: 298
    11.3.3: Manual testing: 299
    11.3.4: Debugging: 299
    11.3.5: Refactoring: 300
    11.3.6: Re-testing: 301

11.4: DEPLOYMENT AND DISTRIBUTION: 302

    11.4.1: Distribute the source code: 302
    11.4.2: Create a Python package: 302
    11.4.3: Package the application as an executable: 304

11.5: CHAPTER 11 CONCLUSION 305

CHAPTER 12: NEXT STEPS IN YOUR PYTHON JOURNEY 306

12.1: ADVANCED PYTHON TOPICS 307

12.2: POPULAR PYTHON LIBRARIES 308

- 12.3: PYTHON IN WEB DEVELOPMENT, DATA SCIENCE, AND MORE 309
- 12.4: ONLINE RESOURCES AND COMMUNITIES 311
- CHAPTER 12 CONCLUSION 314
- WHERE TO CONTINUE? 315
- SEE YOU SOON! 317
- KNOW MORE ABOUT US 319

Who we are

Welcome to this book created by Cuantum Technologies. We are a team of passionate developers who are committed to creating software that delivers creative experiences and solves real-world problems. Our focus is on building high-quality web applications that provide a seamless user experience and meet the needs of our clients.

At our company, we believe that programming is not just about writing code. It's about solving problems and creating solutions that make a difference in people's lives. We are constantly exploring new technologies and techniques to stay at the forefront of the industry, and we are excited to share our knowledge and experience with you through this book.

Our approach to software development is centered around collaboration and creativity. We work closely with our clients to understand their needs and create solutions that are tailored to their specific requirements. We believe that software should be intuitive, easy to use, and visually appealing, and we strive to create applications that meet these criteria.

In this book, we aim to provide you with a practical and hands-on approach to practice Python programming. Whether you are a beginner with no programming experience or an experienced programmer looking to expand your skills, this book is designed to help you develop your skills and build a solid foundation in Python programming.

Our Philosophy:

At the heart of Cuantum, we believe that the best way to create software is through collaboration and creativity. We value the input of our clients, and we work closely with them to create solutions that meet their needs. We also believe that software should be intuitive, easy to use, and visually appealing, and we strive to create applications that meet these criteria.

We also believe that programming is a skill that can be learned and developed over time. We encourage our developers to explore new technologies and techniques, and we provide them with the tools and resources they need to stay at the forefront of the industry. We also believe that programming should be fun and rewarding, and we strive to create a work environment that fosters creativity and innovation.

Our Expertise:

At our software company, we specialize in building web applications that deliver creative experiences and solve real-world problems. Our developers have expertise in a wide range of programming languages and frameworks, including Python, Django, React, Three.js, and Vue.js, among others. We are constantly exploring new technologies and techniques to stay at the forefront of the industry, and we pride ourselves on our ability to create solutions that meet our clients' needs.

We also have extensive experience in data analysis and visualization, machine learning, and artificial intelligence. We believe that these technologies have the potential to transform the way we live and work, and we are excited to be at the forefront of this revolution.

In conclusion, our company is focused on creating software web for creative experiences and solving real-world problems. We believe in collaboration and creativity, and we strive to create solutions that are intuitive, easy to use, and visually appealing. We are passionate about programming, and we are excited to share our knowledge and experience with you through this book. Whether you are a beginner or an experienced programmer, we hope that you find this book to be a valuable resource in your journey to become a proficient Python programmer.

Introduction

Welcome to your journey into the world of Python programming! This book is designed to be your comprehensive guide to learning Python, one of the most popular and versatile programming languages in use today. Whether you're a complete beginner or an experienced programmer looking to expand your skillset, this book has something for everyone. By the time you reach the end, you will have gained a solid understanding of Python and its applications, as well as the confidence to tackle a wide range of programming challenges.

Python is known for its simplicity, readability, and ease of use, making it an ideal choice for both newcomers and seasoned developers alike. It is a powerful, high-level, general-purpose programming language that is used in various domains, including web development, data analysis, artificial intelligence, scientific computing, and more. Its versatility and robustness have contributed to its immense popularity, which continues to grow year after year.

This book will start by introducing you to the basics of Python programming. You will learn about Python's history, its key features, and the reasons behind its widespread adoption. We will then guide you through the process of setting up your Python development environment, ensuring that you have all the necessary tools to start coding right away.

The first few chapters will focus on building a strong foundation in Python, covering essential concepts like data types, variables, operators, control structures, and loops. We will also introduce you to Python's standard library, which provides a wealth of built-in functions and modules that can greatly simplify your programming tasks.

Once you have a solid understanding of the fundamentals, we will move on to more advanced topics, such as functions, file handling, and working with external libraries. You will learn how to create reusable code by defining your own functions, as well as how to read and write files, which are essential skills for any programmer.

Next, we will dive into the world of data structures and algorithms, exploring Python's built-in data structures like lists, tuples, sets, and dictionaries. You will also learn about common algorithms and techniques used in programming, giving you the tools to solve complex problems efficiently.

As we progress further, we will introduce you to object-oriented programming (OOP), a programming paradigm that allows you to create reusable, modular code by defining classes and objects. You will learn about the fundamental concepts of OOP, such as inheritance, polymorphism, and encapsulation, and how to apply them in your Python projects.

Another critical aspect of programming is error handling and exceptions, which will be covered in detail in this book. You will learn how to identify, handle, and resolve errors in your code, ensuring that your programs run smoothly and reliably.

To ensure that you become a well-rounded Python developer, we will also cover best practices for writing clean, maintainable code. This includes adhering to the PEP 8 style guide, using proper naming conventions, commenting and documenting your code, and focusing on code reusability and modularization.

Towards the end of the book, we will walk you through building a real-world application, a task management system called TaskMaster. This project will allow you to apply the concepts and techniques you have learned throughout the book, giving you hands-on experience in designing, implementing, testing, and deploying a Python application.

Finally, we will discuss some advanced Python topics, popular libraries, and various domains where Python is widely used, such as web development and data science. We will also provide you with valuable resources and suggestions on how to continue learning and growing as a Python programmer.

Throughout this book, we will include practical exercises and examples to help reinforce your understanding of the concepts covered. These exercises will not only test your knowledge but also give you the opportunity to practice and apply what you've learned in a hands-on manner.

In conclusion, this book aims to provide you with a thorough and engaging introduction to Python programming, equipping you with the knowledge and skills necessary to become a proficient Python developer. By following the progression of topics, completing the practical exercises, and working through the real-world project, you will gain a deep understanding of Python's capabilities and its applications in various domains.

Our goal is to ensure that you not only learn the syntax and constructs of Python but also develop a strong sense of programming logic, problem-solving techniques, and best practices that will serve you well in your programming career. As you progress through the book, you will find yourself increasingly confident in your ability to write clean, efficient, and maintainable Python code, as well as tackle a diverse range of programming challenges.

As a beginner, it's important to remember that learning to program is a gradual process that requires patience, persistence, and practice. By dedicating time and effort to mastering the material presented in this book, you will steadily develop your programming skills and be well on your way to becoming a proficient Python developer.

We hope that this book not only serves as a valuable resource in your Python learning journey but also sparks a passion for programming and encourages you to explore the many possibilities that Python has to offer. The world of programming is vast and exciting, and with Python as your foundation, you'll be well-prepared to face the challenges and opportunities that lie ahead.

So, let's embark on this exciting journey together and unlock the power of Python programming. Happy coding!

CHAPTER 1: Introduction to Python

1.1 Python: A Versatile and Beginner-friendly Programming Language

Python is a high-level programming language that has been gaining popularity for over three decades now. Created by Guido van Rossum in 1991, Python offers a perfect blend of simplicity and readability, making it an excellent choice for programmers ranging from beginners to experts.

Apart from its simplicity and readability, Python is a versatile language that can be used across various domains, including web development, data analysis, artificial intelligence, machine learning, scientific computing, and more. The language has evolved from being a mere scripting language to a general-purpose language with a rich ecosystem of libraries and frameworks that enable developers to build complex applications and systems quickly and efficiently.

In addition to the standard libraries, Python has numerous third-party libraries, such as NumPy, Pandas, TensorFlow, Django, Flask, and PyTorch, that have gained immense popularity in recent years. These libraries have made it possible for developers to build sophisticated applications and systems with ease. Furthermore, Python's community is known for its active participation in open-source projects, which has led to the development of several innovative libraries and tools.

Some of the key features that make Python beginner-friendly and versatile include:

1. **Easy-to-read syntax**: Python's syntax is designed to be simple and easy to understand. It focuses on readability, which enables programmers to write clear and concise code. Python's use of indentation instead of braces or brackets for code blocks makes it more visually appealing and easier to follow.

2. **High-level language**: Python is a high-level language, which means it abstracts many of the complexities of working with low-level programming languages, such as memory management. This allows developers to focus on the logic of their application rather than dealing with intricate details of the underlying hardware.

3. **Cross-platform compatibility**: Python runs on various platforms, including Windows, macOS, Linux, and Unix, making it a versatile choice for developers. With Python, you

can write code once and run it on multiple platforms without needing to make significant changes.

4. **Extensive standard library**: Python comes with a comprehensive standard library that provides built-in support for many common programming tasks, such as working with files, regular expressions, networking, and more. This reduces the need to write code from scratch or rely on external libraries for basic functionalities.

5. **Strong community support**: Python has a large and active community of developers who contribute to its growth and development. This community creates and maintains a vast number of open-source libraries, tools, and frameworks, making it easier for developers to find solutions to their problems or extend Python's capabilities.

6. **Wide range of applications**: Python's flexibility and versatility make it suitable for various applications, from simple scripting tasks to complex web applications, data analysis, and machine learning. Its adaptability has made it a popular choice among professionals in different industries, including finance, healthcare, and scientific research.

In summary, Python is an excellent choice for beginners and experienced developers alike due to its simplicity, versatility, and strong community support. Its easy-to-read syntax, cross-platform compatibility, and extensive standard library make it a powerful tool for various applications in web development, data science, artificial intelligence, and more. Throughout this book, you will learn more about Python's features and capabilities while building a solid foundation in programming concepts and best practices.

1.2 A little bit of Python's History and Guido van Rossum's Role in its Development

Python's history dates back to the late 1980s, with Guido van Rossum playing a pivotal role in its inception and development. Born in the Netherlands, van Rossum was a computer scientist and a member of the Centrum Wiskunde & Informatica (CWI), the national research institute for mathematics and computer science in the Netherlands.

Python's development began in December 1989 when van Rossum was looking for a hobby project to keep him occupied during the Christmas holidays. Inspired by his work on the ABC language, a teaching language developed at CWI, he set out to create a new scripting language that would be easy to use, understand, and maintain. He named the language "Python" after the British comedy series "Monty Python's Flying Circus," which he enjoyed for its humor and irreverence.

The first version of Python, Python 0.9.0, was released in February 1991. This initial release already featured several core components that are still integral to Python today, such as the use of indentation for code blocks, basic data types, and support for defining functions. Over the years, Python has gone through various iterations and improvements, with key milestones including:

- Python 1.0 (January 1994): This version introduced several important features, such as support for modules, which allowed developers to organize code into reusable components. It also included tools like lambda, map, and filter functions, which enabled more powerful functional programming capabilities.

- Python 2.0 (October 2000): Python 2.0 was a significant step forward in the language's development, bringing new features like list comprehensions and garbage collection. It also introduced Unicode support, making it easier for developers to work with international character sets.

- Python 3.0 (December 2008): Python 3.0, also known as "Python 3000" or "Py3K," was a major release that aimed to fix several longstanding issues in the language. It introduced numerous changes, including revised syntax, improved standard library modules, and better Unicode support. However, it was not backward compatible with Python 2.x, which initially slowed down its adoption.

Since the release of Python 3.0, the language has continued to evolve, with new features and improvements being added regularly. Python 2.x was officially retired in January 2020, with Python 3.x now being the recommended version for all new projects.

Guido van Rossum served as Python's Benevolent Dictator For Life (BDFL), a title given to him by the Python community, for nearly three decades. In this role, he was the final authority on decisions related to the language's design and development. In July 2018, van Rossum announced his retirement from active involvement in Python and stepped down as BDFL. The Python community has since transitioned to a more democratic governance model, with a steering council guiding the language's future development.

Python's growth can be attributed not only to Guido van Rossum's vision and dedication but also to the vibrant and active community that has grown around the language. Today, Python is one of the most popular programming languages worldwide, with a diverse range of applications across multiple industries.

1.3 Differences between Python 2.x and Python 3.x

Python has evolved significantly over the years, with two major versions – Python 2.x and Python 3.x – being the most prominent. Python 3.x was introduced in 2008, with the aim of addressing and improving upon various design flaws and inconsistencies present in Python 2.x. However, Python 3.x was not backward compatible with Python 2.x, which led to a slow adoption of the new version initially. Nonetheless, Python 3.x is now the recommended version for all new projects, and Python 2.x reached its end of life in January 2020.

Here are some of the key differences between Python 2.x and Python 3.x, emphasizing the advantages of using Python 3.x:

1. Print function: In Python 2.x, print is a statement, whereas, in Python 3.x, it is a function. This change promotes consistency with other functions and requires the use of parentheses around the arguments in Python 3.x.

Python 2.x:

```
print "Hello, World!"
```

Code block: 1.1

Python 3.x:

```
print("Hello, World!")
```

Code block: 1.2

2. Integer division: In Python 2.x, dividing two integers results in an integer, with the result being truncated. In Python 3.x, dividing two integers results in a float, which is a more intuitive behavior.

Python 2.x:

```
result = 5 / 2  # result is 2
```

Code block: 1.3

Python 3.x:

```
result = 5 / 2  # result is 2.5
```

Code block: 1.4

3. **Unicode support**: Python 3.x has improved Unicode support, making it easier to work with international character sets. In Python 3.x, all strings are Unicode by default, while in Python 2.x, strings are ASCII by default.

4. **Range function**: In Python 2.x, the range() function returns a list, while in Python 3.x, it returns a range object, which is more memory-efficient, especially for large ranges.

5. **Iterators instead of lists**: Python 3.x uses iterators for many built-in functions that used to return lists in Python 2.x, such as zip(), map(), and filter(). This change improves memory efficiency, as iterators generate values one at a time instead of creating a full list in memory.

6. **Keyword-only arguments**: Python 3.x introduced keyword-only arguments, which allow specifying certain function arguments as keyword-only, making it mandatory for the caller to provide them using keyword syntax. This feature makes function calls more readable and helps prevent errors due to incorrect argument order.

7. **Improved exception handling**: Python 3.x made changes to the syntax for exception handling, such as using the 'as' keyword to assign the exception to a variable. This change promotes more consistent and cleaner code.

Python 2.x:

```
try:
    # some code
except ValueError, e:
    # handle exception
```

Code block: 1.5

Python 3.x:

```
try:
    # some code
except ValueError as e:
    # handle exception
```

Code block: 1.6

In conclusion, Python 3.x is a significant upgrade over Python 2.x in terms of language design, consistency, and performance. Some of the key improvements include support for Unicode as the default string type, enhanced support for iterators and generators, and better handling of exceptions. Additionally, Python 3.x introduces several new features, such as the "asyncio" module for asynchronous programming, advanced type hinting capabilities, and improved performance optimizations.

Given these benefits, it is highly recommended that developers migrate from Python 2.x to Python 3.x for all new projects. Moreover, by using Python 3.x, developers can take advantage of the latest and most up-to-date features of the language, ensuring that their code is as efficient and effective as possible.

Throughout this book, we will be focusing exclusively on Python 3.x, providing you with a comprehensive understanding of the language and its capabilities. By the end of this book, you will be equipped with the skills and knowledge necessary to build robust, scalable, and efficient applications using Python 3.x.

1.4 Installing Python and Setting Up a Development Environment

To get started with Python programming, you need to install Python and set up a development environment using an Integrated Development Environment (IDE) or a code editor. In this section, we will guide you through the process of installing Python and setting up popular IDEs like PyCharm, Visual Studio Code (VSCode), and Jupyter Notebook.

1.4.1 Installing Python

Step 1: Go to www.python.org

Step 2: Select 'Downloads' from the toolbar

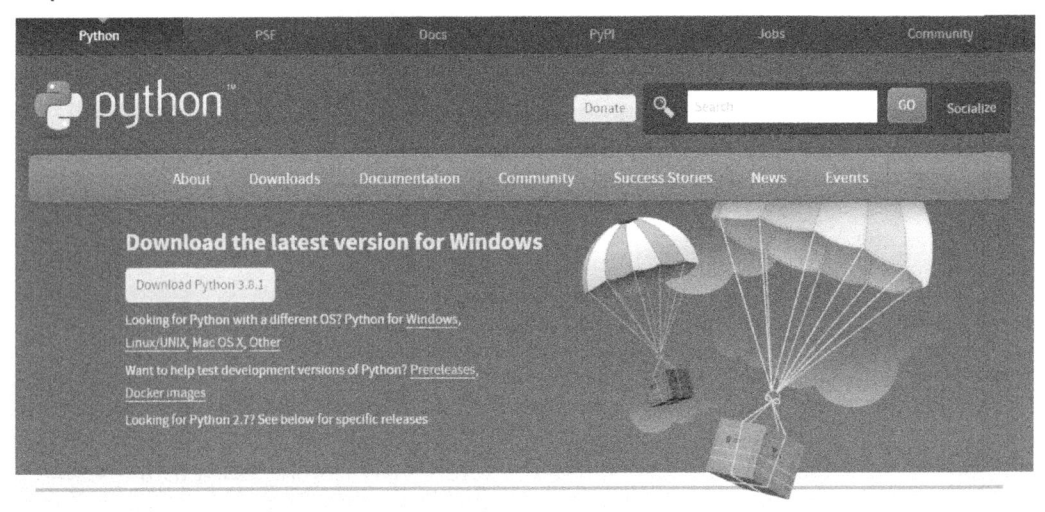

Step 3: Click on 'Download Python 3.8.1' or the latest version available

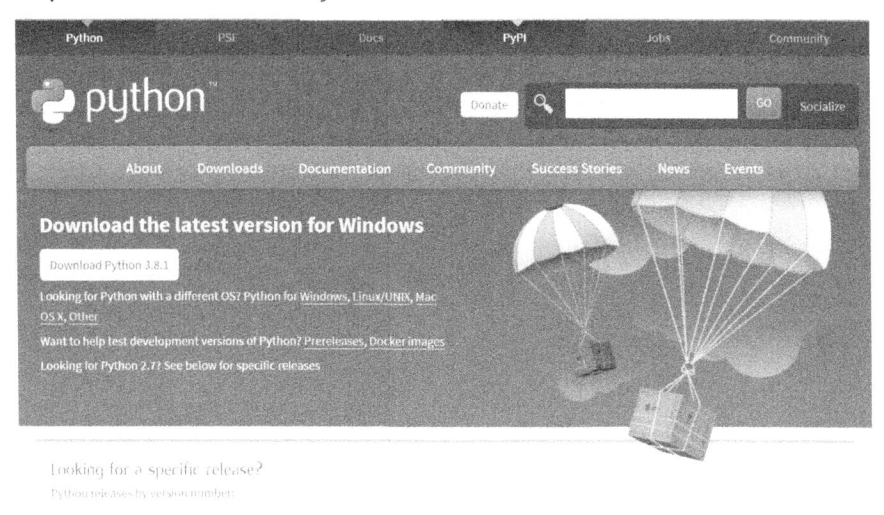

Step 4: Then, go to the **Fil**e option. After that, a security dialog box will appear as shown below. Click on 'Run' to continue the installation process

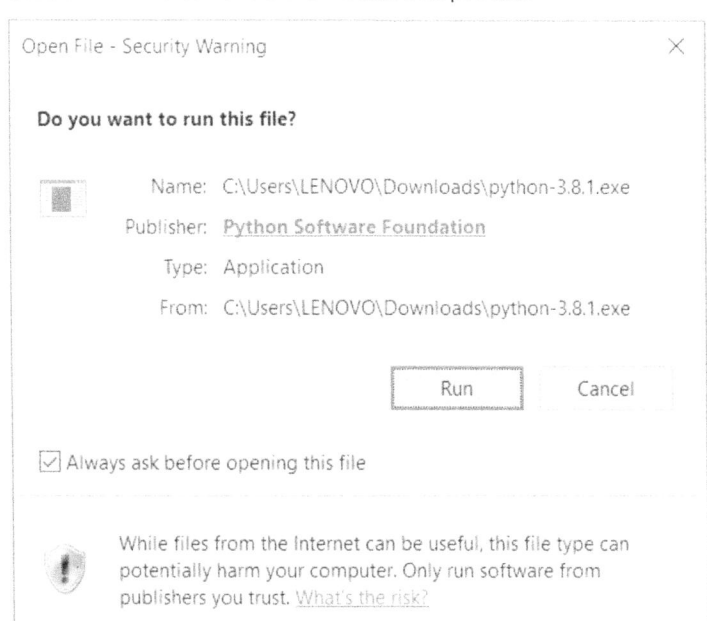

Step 5: Click on 'Install Now'

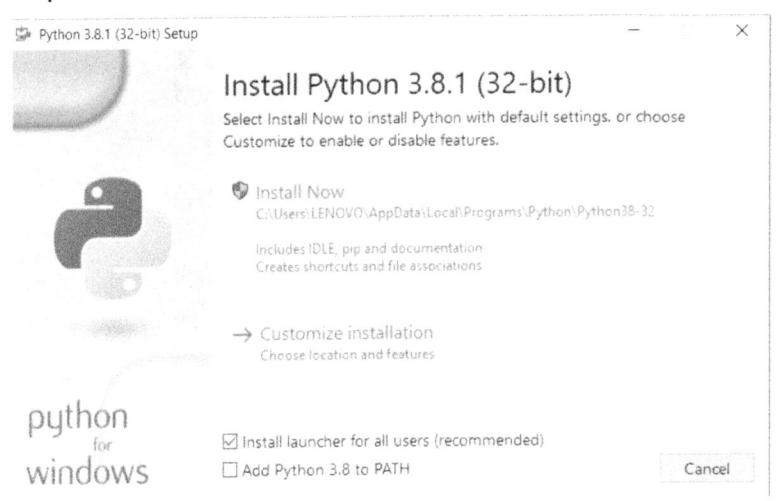

Once you do that, you can see the setup in progress as in the below screenshot:

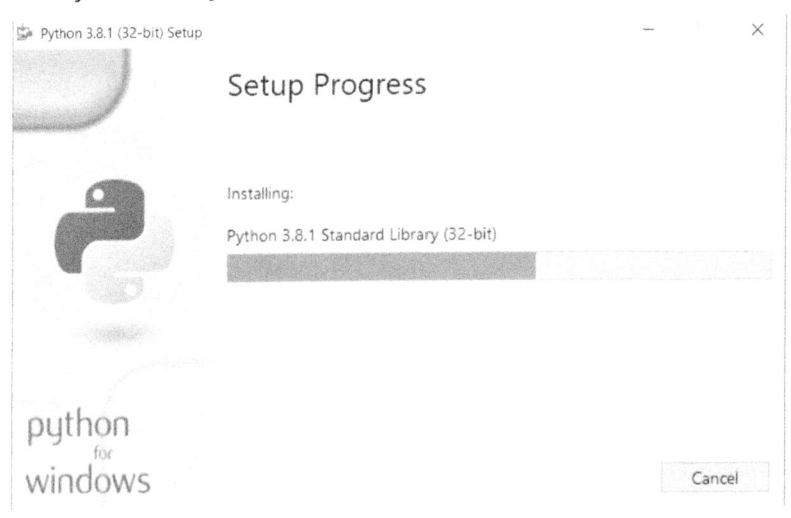

Step 6: After the installation of Python, when you see a window with the message 'Setup was successful', click on the 'Close' button.

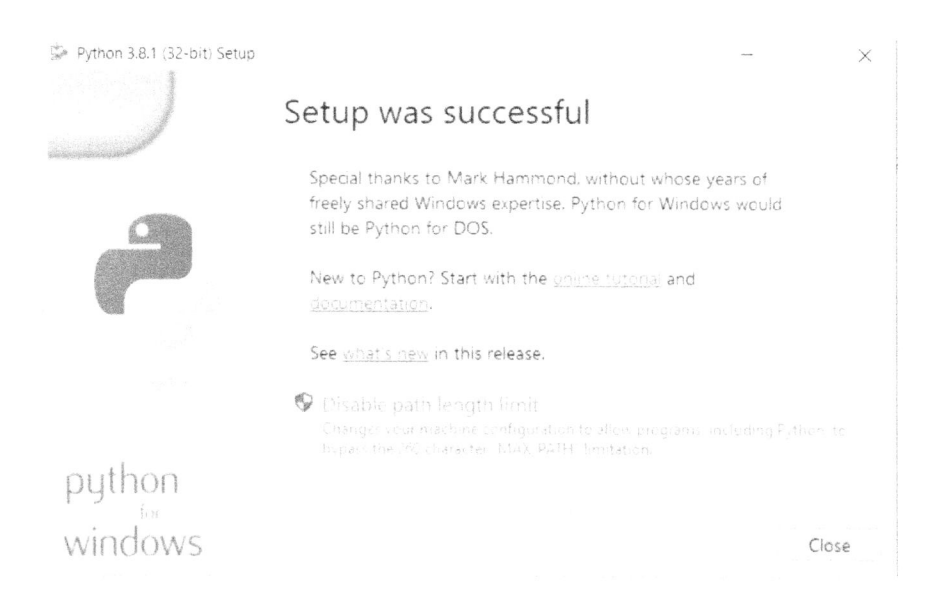

Now, you are ready with Python 3.8.1 installed in your system.

Further, we will move on to the installation of PyCharm.

1.4.2 Setting Up a Development Environment

There are several IDEs and code editors available for Python development. Here, we'll discuss setting up three popular options: PyCharm, Visual Studio Code (VSCode), and Jupyter Notebook.

PyCharm

Step 1: To download PyCharm, visit the official website of JetBrains: http://www.jetbrains.com/pycharm/

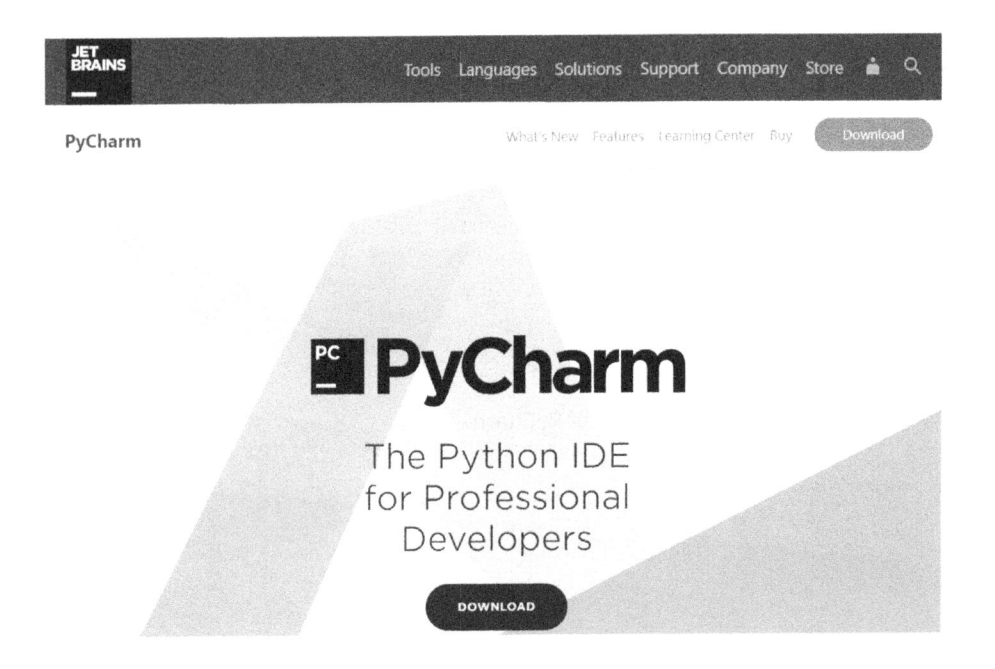

Step 2: Click on the 'Download" button

Step 3: After that, you will see the below window with two options, **Professional** and **Community**

Step 4: Download the **Community** version

Note: If you are interested to work with the Professional version, then you can download the **Professional** version and avail a free trial.

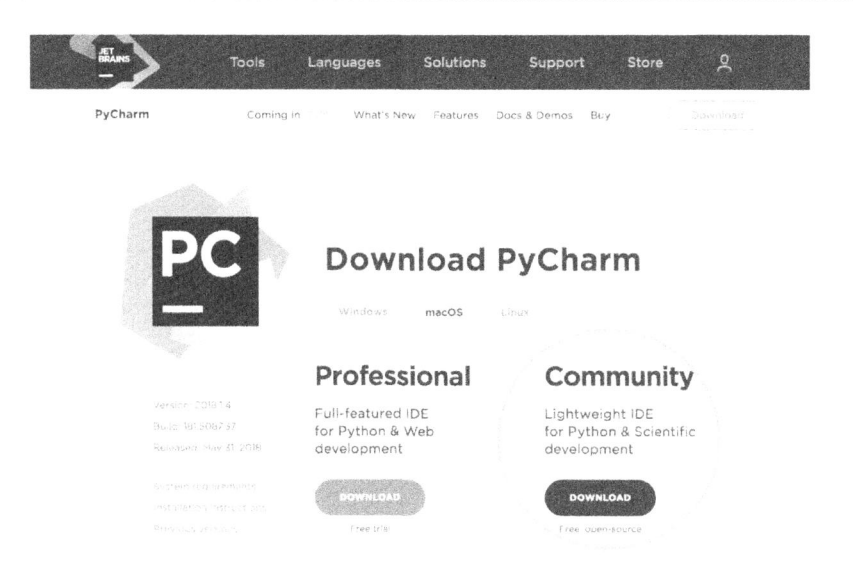

Step 5: After downloading the file, click on it

Step 6: When the following window appears, click on **Next** and the installation process will start

Step 7: After clicking on **Next**, first, a window for setting up the installation location will appear.

Note: You can either select a folder for the installation location or retain the default path.

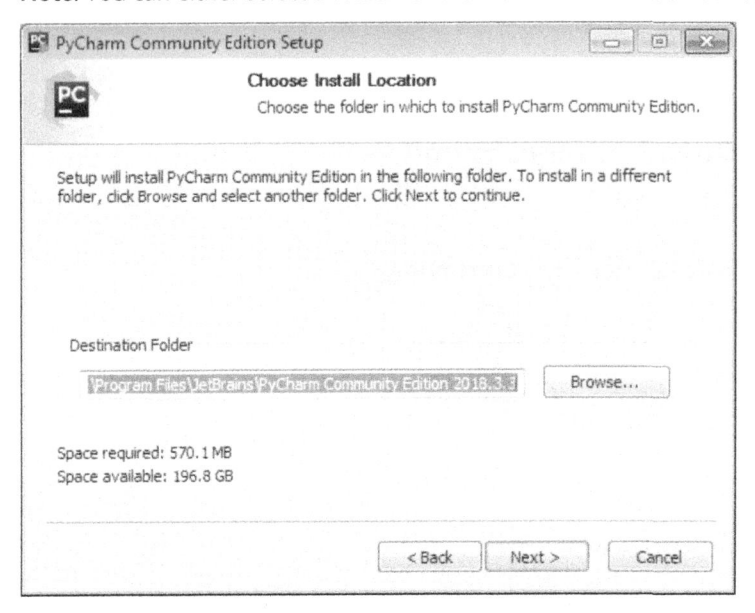

Step 8: In the next step, you can set the **Installation Options** as per requirements, and then, click on the **Next** button to proceed

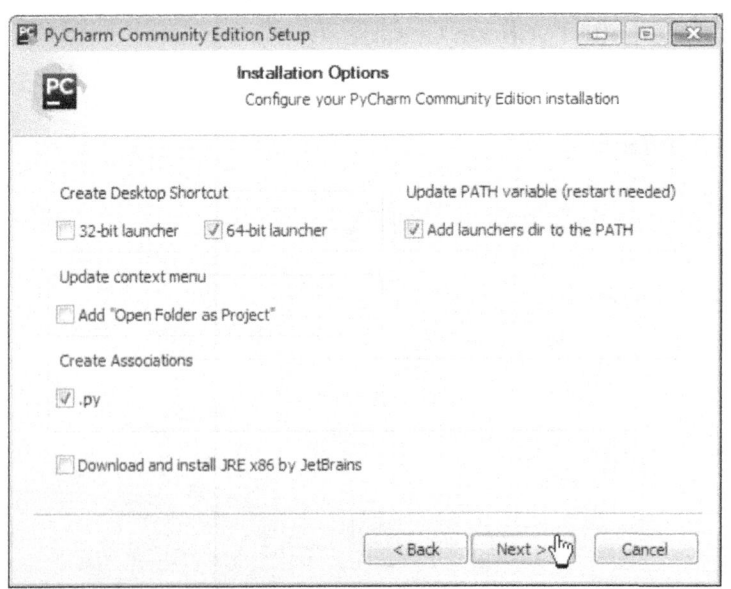

Step 9: Now, you have to select the Start Menu folder, or you can leave it as default

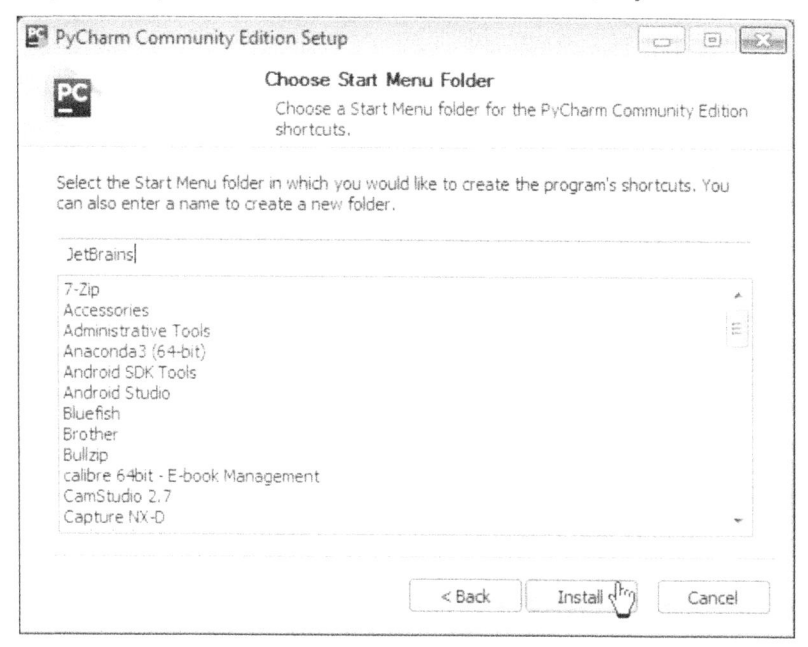

Step 10: After these steps, click on the **Install** button as above to start the installation process

Step 11: When you click on the Finish button, your PyCharm installation completes

Now, you have successfully installed PyCharm and Python both in your system.

Configuring PyCharm

The first time PyCharm launches, it will offer you the chance to import older settings (from a previous PyCharm installation).

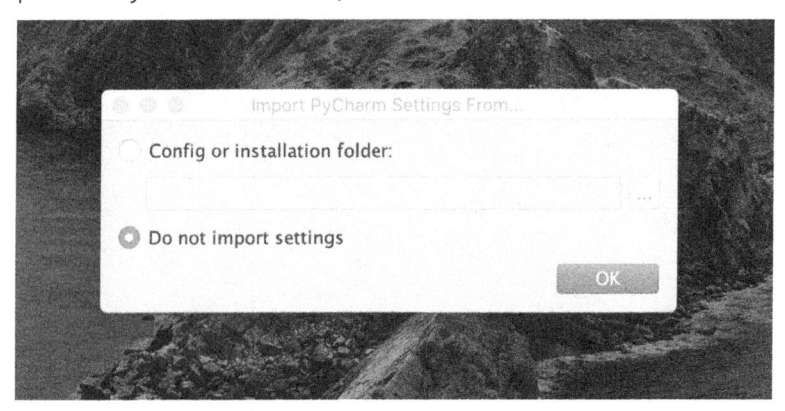

If you are installing PyCharm for the first time, you don't need to import settings. The next screen will ask you to customize PyCharm. The first question is to select a keymap scheme. Keymap scheme refers to keyboard shortcuts, check the different examples in the figure. You can leave it as it if you never used PyCharm before, and it is updated for newer Mac OS versions.

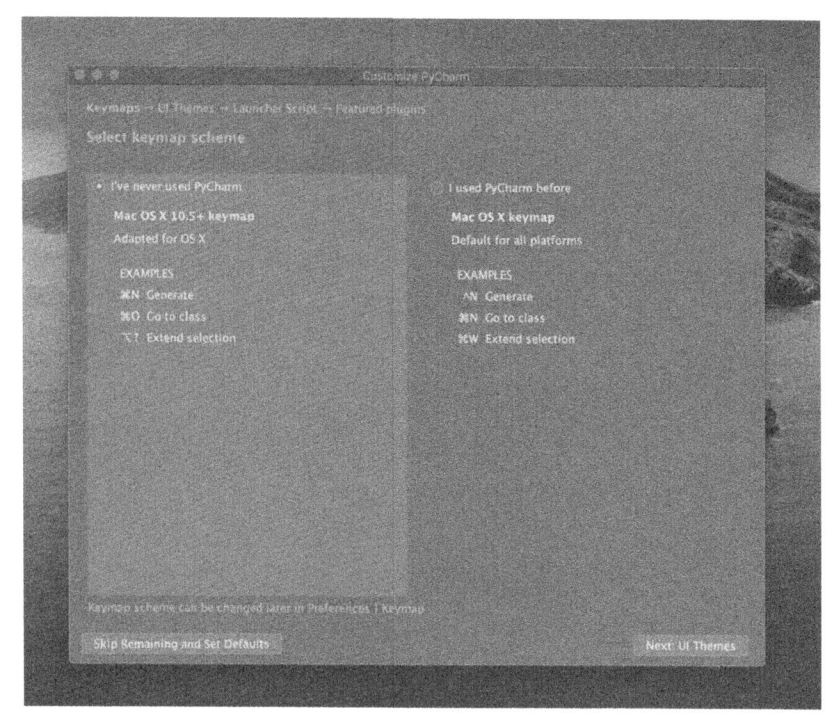

I click on Next: UI Themes. On the following page, I opted for the dark 'Darcula' theme. Don't be disappointed if you don't like any of the themes right now. Later you can add a plugin that allows you to choose between several other beautiful options 😊 *(hint: it's a plugin called Material UI Theme)*. After you chose, click on Next: Launcher Script. A Launcher script adds a small terminal program that can launch PyCharm from your terminal in any given directory. What I mean is that it allows you to do the following:

charm ~/DeveloperProjects/MyNewPythonApplication

In that line, I am launching PyCharm in the directory called 'MyNewPythonApplication' that is a sub-directory of 'DeveloperProjects.' If you like this feature, check the box. To continue, click on Next: Featured plugins.

PYTHON PROGRAMMING UNLOCKED FOR BEGINNERS

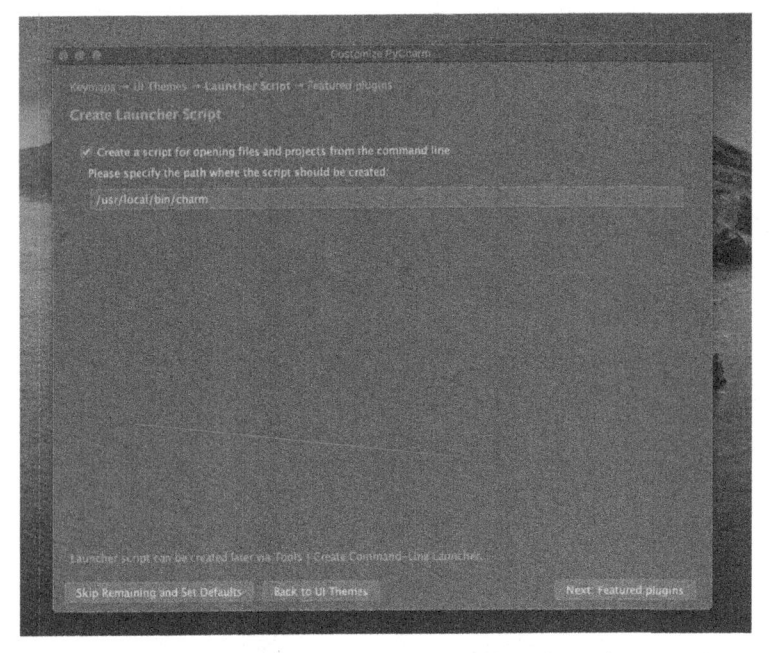

On the next screen, Pycharm suggests popular plugins. That's a personal choice. The configuration is almost ready, now click on Start using PyCharm.

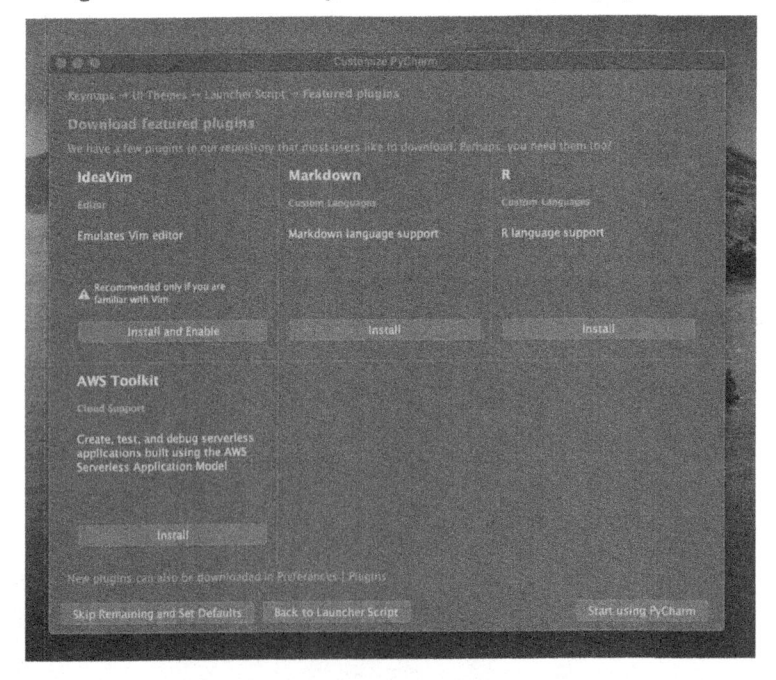

books.cuantum.tech

Creating a new project in PyCharm

Now, the next step is to either open an old project (from a repository on your local machine or version control) or create a new project. Let's suppose you want to start a new project. Then, click on + Create New Project.

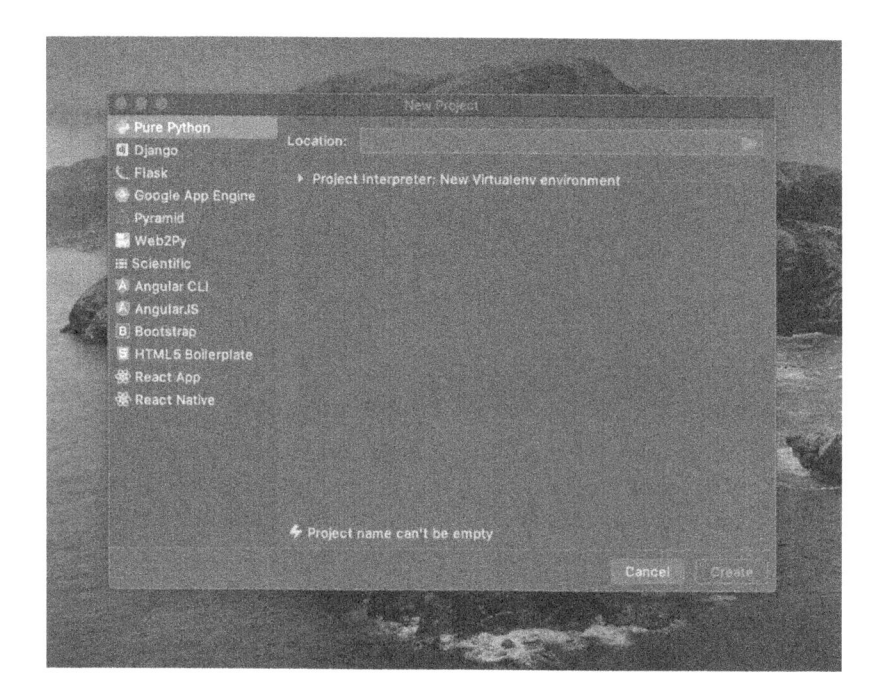

If you chose the professional version of PyCharm, you can select among several project options from the left sidebar. Or, in case you have the free version, you won't have these options, so you can only open a new Pure Python project. You can create a new project in the same way, though. Chose the location (directory) where you want to save your project.

By clicking on Project Interpreter: New Virtualenv environment, you can choose the environment options for your new project. When you are coding in Python, you will probably make use of several libraries. The environment will hold all the libraries you will install for that project. There are two options 1) New environment or 2) Existing interpreter.

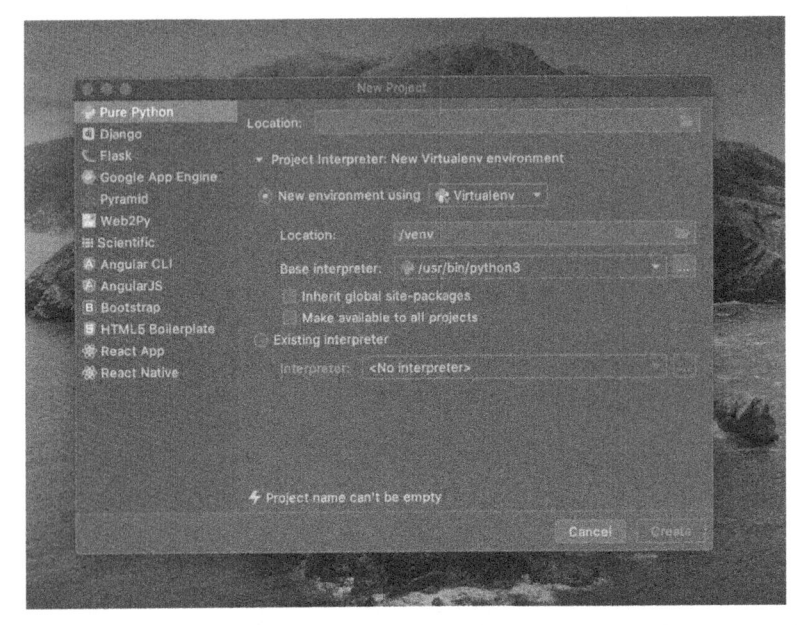

The new environment (first) option gives yet three possibilities, Virtualenv, Pipenv, or Conda. Virtualenv is the default option. Pipenv is newer, and it is supposed to have extra functionalities. To make use of Conda, you need to have installed the Anaconda or Miniconda on your machine. You can use the default Virtualenv. Besides, you can choose the Base interpreter (Python 3 recommended). Click on Create to continue.

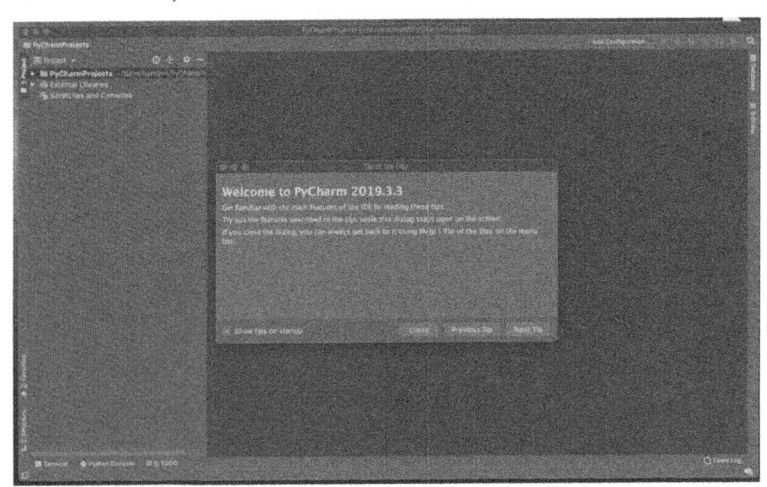

Before you can start coding, PyCharm suggests a 'Tip of the Day' option with tricks on how to increase your productivity by using keyboard shortcuts. If you think you don't need them, you can uncheck this option on the bottom left corner of the pop-up. After that, close the pop-up.

Now you can create a new file by clicking Cmd + N (on Mac) or clicking on File > New > File or clicking File > New > Python File (from templates). If you chose the last option, PyCharm will create a file with the .py extension.

You can finally write your code! After you are ready, you can run your script by clicking Run on the main menu (the green arrow on the top right corner) or pressing Ctrl + Option + R on the keyboard. PyCharm offers several features to help you code.

Visual Studio Code (VSCode)

Getting up and running with *Visual Studio Code* is swift and straightforward. It is a small download so you can install it quickly and give the VS Code a try. VS Code is a free code editor. Additionally, it runs on the *macOS, Linux, and Windows* operating systems. Let's see how we can set up the same in the different platforms we use.

The first step is shared across all the platforms irrespective of any OS you are using.

Download Visual Studio Code:

You can download Visual Studio code from URL *"https://code.visualstudio.com/download"* by selecting the right platform:

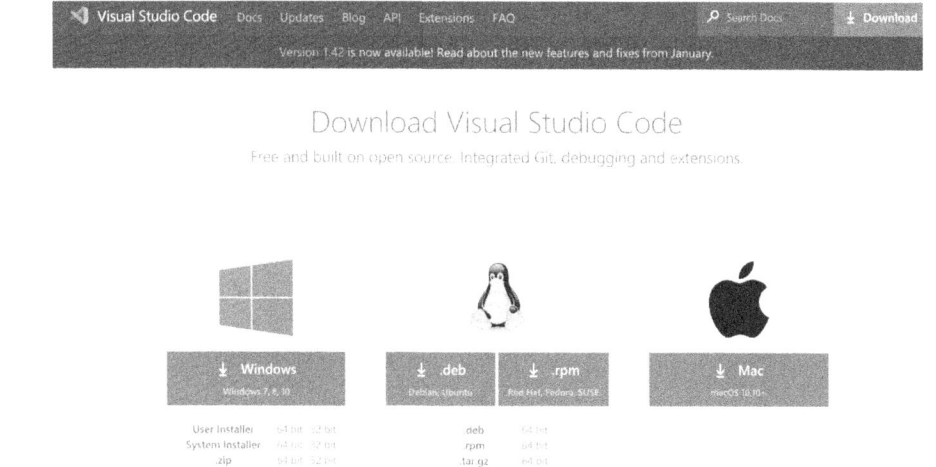

You can click any of the icons mentioned above, depending on the operating system for which you are planning to download the visual studio code editor.

How to install Visual Studio Code on macOS?

Follow the below steps*(shown in gif file and mentioned in bullet points)* to install the VS Code on macOS:

1. *Download Visual Studio Code for macOS.*
2. *After clicking on the Mac option on the download site, it will download a zip file, as shown below:*
3. *Double-click on the downloaded zip to expand the contents. It will give a file, as shown below:*
4. *Drag **"Visual Studio Code.app"** to the **"Applications"** folder, so as it available in the **"Launchpad."***
5. *Double click on the **"Visual Studio Code"** to open.*
6. *Add VS Code to your Dock by right-clicking on the icon to bring up the context menu and choosing **Options => Keep in Dock.***

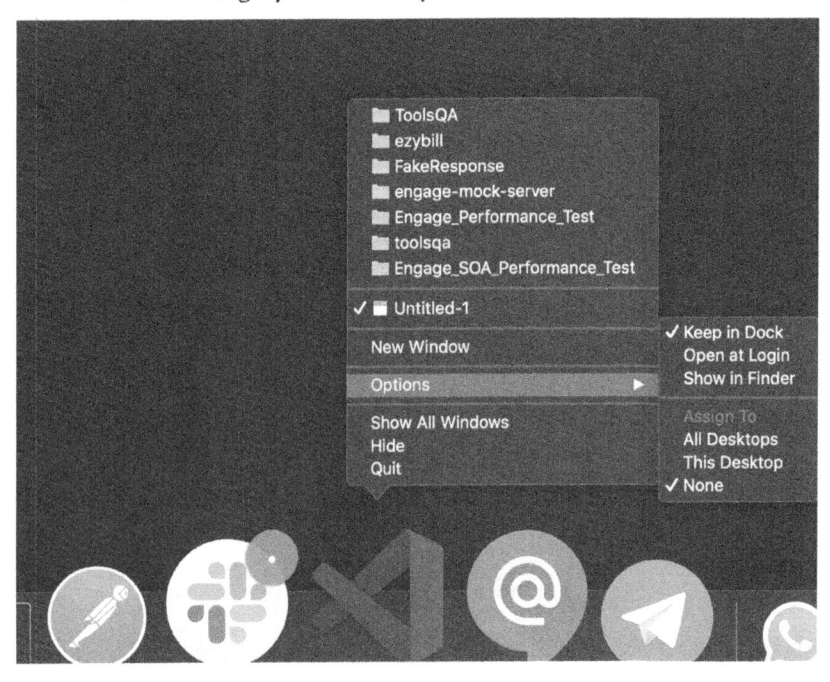

How to Install Visual Studio Code on Windows?

Firstly, download the Visual Studio Code installer for Windows. Once it is downloaded, run the installer *(VSCodeUserSetup-{version}.exe)*. It will only take a minute.

Secondly, accept the agreement and click on next.

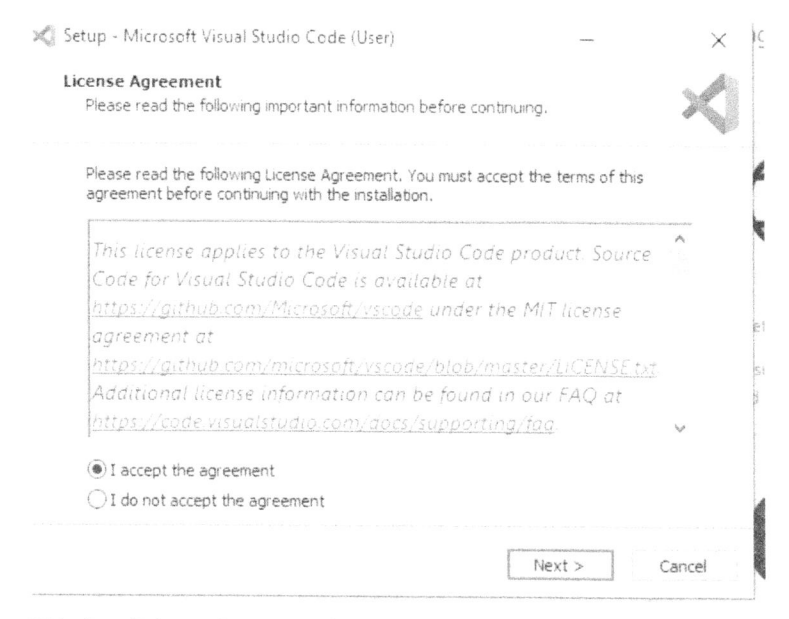

Thirdly, click on *"create a desktop icon"* so that it can be accessed from desktop and click on Next.

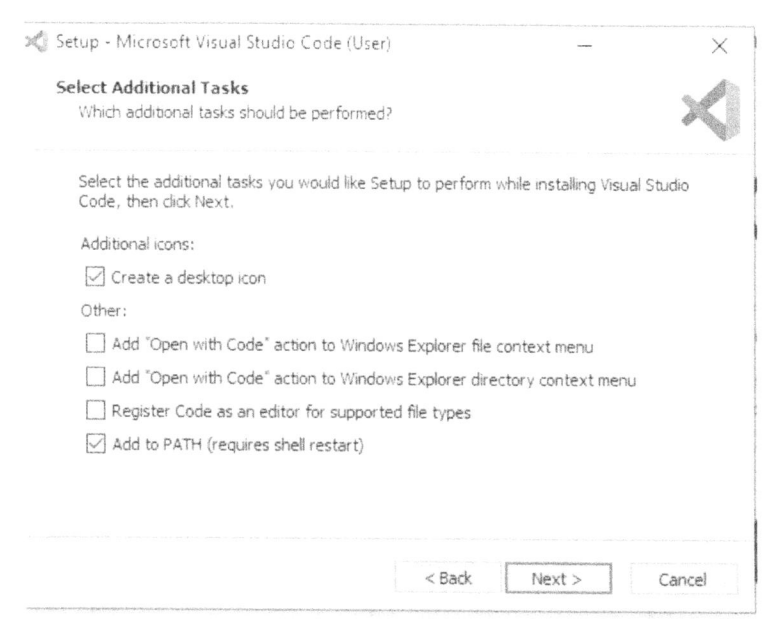

After that, click on the install button.

PYTHON PROGRAMMING UNLOCKED FOR BEGINNERS

Setup - Microsoft Visual Studio Code (User)

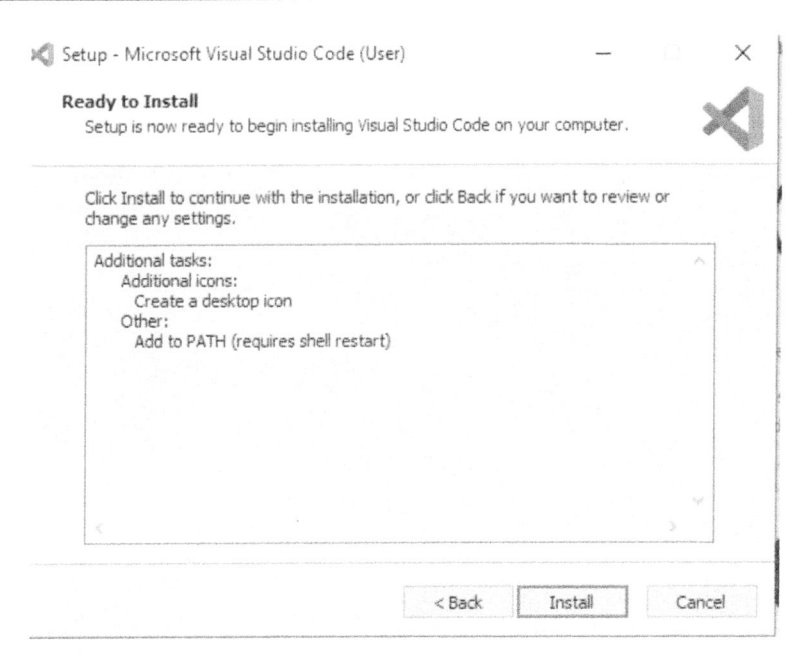

Ready to Install
Setup is now ready to begin installing Visual Studio Code on your computer.

Click Install to continue with the installation, or click Back if you want to review or change any settings.

```
Additional tasks:
    Additional icons:
        Create a desktop icon
    Other:
        Add to PATH (requires shell restart)
```

< Back   Install   Cancel

Finally, after installation completes, click on the finish button, and the visual studio code will get open.

Setup - Microsoft Visual Studio Code (User)

Completing the Visual Studio Code Setup Wizard

Setup has finished installing Visual Studio Code on your computer. The application may be launched by selecting the installed icons.

Click Finish to exit Setup.

☑ Launch Visual Studio Code

Finish

By default, VS Code installs under C:\users{username}\AppData\Local\Programs\Microsoft VS Code.

books.cuantum.tech

After the successful installation, let's move to the next section to understand the various components of the User Interface of Visual Studio Code Editor.

What are the essential components of the VS Code?

Visual Studio Code is a code editor at its core. Like many other code editors, VS Code adopts a standard user interface and layout of an explorer on the left, showing all of the files and folders you have access to. Additionally, it has an editor on the right, showing the content of the files you have opened. Below are a few of the most critical components the VSCode editor:

VS Code comes with a straight-forward and intuitive layout that maximizes the space provided for the editor while leaving ample room to browse. Additionally, it allows access to the full context of your folder or project. The UI is divided into five areas, as highlighted in the above image.

1. *Editor* - *It is the main area to edit your files. You can open as many editors as possible side by side vertically and horizontally.*
2. *SideBar* - *Contains different views like the Explorer to assist you while working on your project.*
3. *Status Bar* - *It contains the information about the opened project and the files you edit.*
4. *Activity Bar* - *It is located on the far left-hand side. It lets you switch between views and gives you additional context-specific indicators, like the number of outgoing changes when Git is enabled.*
5. *Panels* - *It displays different panels below the editor region for output or debug information, errors, and warnings, or an integrated terminal. Additionally, the panel can also move to the right for more vertical space.*

VS Code opens up in the same state it was last in, every time you start it. It also preserves folder, layout, and opened files.

Jupyter Notebook

1. To install Jupyter Notebook, open a command prompt (Windows) or terminal (macOS or Linux) and run the following command:

```
pip install notebook
```

Code block: 1.7

2. Once the installation is complete, launch Jupyter Notebook by running the following command:

```
jupyter notebook
```

Code block: 1.8

This will open a new browser window with the Jupyter Notebook interface.

3. To create a new Python notebook, click on "New" in the upper-right corner and select "Python 3" (or the appropriate Python version) from the dropdown menu.
4. You can now write Python code in the notebook cells and execute them by clicking "Run" or pressing **Shift+Enter**. Jupyter Notebook allows you to mix code, text, and multimedia content, making it an excellent tool for interactive data exploration and documentation.

With Python installed and your development environment set up, you're now ready to start writing and executing Python code. Whether you're an experienced programmer or a beginner, the flexibility of the Python language makes it an ideal choice for a wide range of projects. Throughout this book, you can choose to work with any of these development environments (PyCharm, Visual Studio Code, or Jupyter Notebook) based on your personal preference and the nature of the projects you'll be working on.

One of the advantages of working with Python is that it has a large and active community of developers who are constantly creating new libraries, modules, and tools that can be used to extend the language's capabilities. With so many resources available, you're sure to find the tools and frameworks you need to tackle any project. Additionally, Python is known for its readability and ease of use, which makes it a great choice for collaborative projects where multiple programmers are working on the same codebase.

Each development environment also offers unique features and advantages to help you be more productive and efficient in your programming. For example, PyCharm offers advanced debugging tools, while Visual Studio Code has a powerful code editor and Jupyter Notebook allows you to create interactive notebooks that combine code, visualizations, and documentation. No matter which environment you choose, all of them provide a solid foundation for Python programming and will help you to become a more skilled and effective developer

CHAPTER 2: Python Basics

2.1 Python Syntax

Python is well-known for its clean and easy-to-understand syntax, which makes it an ideal language for beginner programmers. As we delve into Python's syntax, you'll notice that it emphasizes readability and simplicity, enabling you to write code that is both efficient and easy to maintain.

2.1.1 Indentation

One of the most significant aspects of Python's syntax is its use of indentation. Instead of relying on curly braces {} or other symbols to denote code blocks, Python uses indentation to define the structure of the code. This enforces consistent formatting and improves code readability.

In Python, you must indent each level of a code block using either spaces or tabs, with a consistent number of spaces or tabs for each level. The most common convention is to use 4 spaces per indentation level.

Consider the following example of an if-else block:

```python
x = 5

if x > 0:
    print("x is positive")
else:
    print("x is non-positive")
```

Code block: 2.1

Here, the statements **print("x is positive")** and **print("x is non-positive")** are indented to indicate that they belong to the if and else blocks, respectively.

2.1.2 Comments

Comments are an essential part of any programming language, as they allow you to add explanations and notes to your code. In Python, you can create comments using the hash symbol (#). Anything following a # on a line is considered a comment and will not be executed by the Python interpreter.

```python
# This is a single-line comment

x = 5  # This is an inline comment

# You can also use comments to
# explain code over multiple lines
```

Code block: 2.2

2.1.3 Variables

In Python, you can create variables by assigning a value to a name using the equal sign (=). Variable names in Python should be descriptive and adhere to the following rules:

- Must start with a letter or an underscore
- Can only contain letters, numbers, or underscores
- Are case-sensitive

Examples of valid variable names are **x**, **counter**, **result**, and **_temp**.

```python
name = "Alice"
age = 30
```

Code block: 2.3

2.1.4 Statements and Expressions

A statement is a single line of code that performs an action, while an expression is a combination of values, variables, and operators that can be evaluated to produce a result.

Examples of statements:

```
x = 5     # assignment statement
print(x)  # function call statement
```

Code block: 2.4

Examples of expressions:

```
3 + 4
x * 2
x > 0
```

Code block: 2.5

2.1.5 Basic Data Types and Operators

Python supports several built-in data types, such as integers, floats, strings, and booleans. It also provides a variety of operators to perform arithmetic, comparison, and logical operations.

Examples:

```python
# Arithmetic operations
x = 5 + 3   # addition
y = 7 - 2   # subtraction
z = 4 * 2   # multiplication
a = 9 / 3   # division

# Comparison operations
b = 5 > 3   # greater than
c = 4 < 2   # less than
d = 5 == 5  # equal to
e = 5 != 3  # not equal to

# Logical operations
f = True and False   # logical AND
g = True or False    # logical OR
h = not True         # logical NOT
```

Code block: 2.6

With this basic understanding of Python's syntax, you are now equipped to start writing simple programs and expressions in Python. As we progress through this book, we will build on these foundational concepts to explore more advanced topics, such as functions, classes, and modules. It's important to become comfortable with Python's syntax, as it will allow you to write clear, efficient, and maintainable code as you develop more complex applications.

Remember that Python emphasizes readability and simplicity, so always strive to write code that is easy to understand and follow. This will not only make your work more enjoyable but will also make it easier for others to read and collaborate on your projects.

Exercise 2.1.1: Calculate the Area of a Rectangle

In this exercise, you will write a simple Python program that calculates the area of a rectangle. You will practice using Python syntax, including variables, expressions, and the **print()** function.

Instructions:

1. Create a new Python file or open a Python interpreter.
2. Declare a variable named **length** and assign it the value of the rectangle's length (e.g., 10).
3. Declare a variable named **width** and assign it the value of the rectangle's width (e.g., 5).
4. Calculate the area of the rectangle by multiplying the **length** and **width** variables, and assign the result to a new variable named **area**.
5. Use the **print()** function to display the area of the rectangle.

Your final code should look something like this:

```python
length = 10
width = 5
area = length * width
print("The area of the rectangle is", area)
```

Code block: E.2.1.1.1

When you run your program, you should see output similar to the following:

```
The area of the rectangle is 50
```

Code block: E.2.1.1.2

Feel free to modify the **length** and **width** values to test your program with different rectangle sizes. This exercise helps you become familiar with Python syntax, including variable assignment, arithmetic expressions, and the **print()** function.

Exercise 2.1.2: Printing a Triangle

In this exercise, you will write a Python program that prints a simple triangle pattern using asterisks. You will practice using the **print()** function and Python syntax.

Instructions:

1. Create a new Python file or open a Python interpreter.
2. Use the **print()** function to display a triangle pattern with the following structure:

```
  *
 ***
*****
```

Code block: E.2.1.2.1

Your final code should look something like this:

```python
print("  *  ")
print(" *** ")
print("*****")
```

Code block: E.2.1.2.2

When you run your program, you should see output similar to the following:

```
  *
 ***
*****
```

Code block: E.2.1.2.3

Exercise 2.1.3: Printing a Multiplication Table

In this exercise, you will write a Python program that prints a multiplication table for a given number. You will practice using the **print()** function and Python syntax.

Instructions:

1. Create a new Python file or open a Python interpreter.
2. Declare a variable named **number** and assign it a value (e.g., 7).
3. Use the **print()** function to display a multiplication table for the given number, up to 10 times the given number.

Your final code should look something like this:

```python
number = 7

print(f"{number} x 1 = {number * 1}")
print(f"{number} x 2 = {number * 2}")
print(f"{number} x 3 = {number * 3}")
print(f"{number} x 4 = {number * 4}")
print(f"{number} x 5 = {number * 5}")
print(f"{number} x 6 = {number * 6}")
print(f"{number} x 7 = {number * 7}")
print(f"{number} x 8 = {number * 8}")
print(f"{number} x 9 = {number * 9}")
print(f"{number} x 10 = {number * 10}")
```

Code block: E.2.1.3.1

When you run your program, you should see output similar to the following:

```
7 x 1 = 7
7 x 2 = 14
7 x 3 = 21
7 x 4 = 28
7 x 5 = 35
7 x 6 = 42
7 x 7 = 49
7 x 8 = 56
7 x 9 = 63
7 x 10 = 70
```

Code block: E.2.1.3.2

Feel free to modify the **number** variable to practice with different multiplication tables. These exercises help you become familiar with Python syntax and the **print()** function.

2.2 Variables and Data Types

In this section, we will discuss variables and data types in Python. Variables are essential in programming as they allow you to store and manipulate data, while data types define the kind of data that can be stored in a variable.

2.2.1 Variables

Variables in Python are used to store values for later use in your program. A variable is assigned a value using the assignment operator (=). The variable name must follow certain naming conventions:

- Start with a letter or an underscore (_)
- Consist of letters, numbers, or underscores
- Be case-sensitive

Examples of variable assignments:

```python
name = "John"
age = 25
_height = 175.5
```

Code block: 2.7

You can also perform multiple assignments in a single line:

```python
x, y, z = 1, 2, 3
```

Code block: 2.8

2.2.2 Data Types

Python has several built-in data types that allow you to work with various forms of data. Some of the most common data types are:

- Integers (int): Whole numbers, such as 5, -3, or 42.
- Floating-point numbers (float): Decimal numbers, such as 3.14, -0.5, or 1.0.
- Strings (str): Sequences of characters, such as "hello", 'world', or "Python is fun!".
- Booleans (bool): Logical values, either **True** or **False**.

You can determine the type of a value or variable using the **type()** function:

```python
x = 42
print(type(x))   # Output: <class 'int'>

y = 3.14
print(type(y))   # Output: <class 'float'>

z = "Python"
print(type(z))   # Output: <class 'str'>

a = True
print(type(a))   # Output: <class 'bool'>
```

Code block: 2.9

2.2.3 Type Conversion

You can convert between different data types using built-in Python functions, such as **int()**, **float()**, **str()**, and **bool()**.

Examples of type conversion:

```
x = 5.5
y = int(x)    # Convert float to int, y becomes 5

a = 3
b = float(a)  # Convert int to float, b becomes 3.0

c = 42
d = str(c)    # Convert int to str, d becomes "42"

e = "123"
f = int(e)    # Convert str to int, f becomes 123
```

Code block: 2.10

It's important to note that not all conversions are possible. For example, converting a non-numeric string to an integer or float will result in a **ValueError**.

Understanding variables and data types is crucial in Python programming, as it forms the basis for manipulating data and performing various operations. As you progress through this book, you will encounter more advanced data types, such as lists, dictionaries, and tuples, which will allow you to work with more complex data structures.

Exercise 2.2.1: Celsius to Fahrenheit Converter

In this exercise, you will write a Python program that converts a temperature in degrees Celsius to degrees Fahrenheit. You will practice using variables, data types, expressions, and the **print()** function.

Instructions:

1. Create a new Python file or open a Python interpreter.
2. Declare a variable named **celsius** and assign it the value of the temperature in degrees Celsius (e.g., 30).
3. Calculate the temperature in degrees Fahrenheit using the formula **fahrenheit = (celsius * 9/5) + 32**, and assign the result to a new variable named **fahrenheit**.
4. Use the **print()** function to display the temperature in degrees Fahrenheit, formatted as a string with a degree symbol (°F).

Your final code should look something like this:

```
celsius = 30
fahrenheit = (celsius * 9/5) + 32
print(f"{celsius}°C is equal to {fahrenheit}°F")
```

Code block: E.2.2.1.1

When you run your program, you should see output similar to the following:

```
30°C is equal to 86.0°F
```

Code block: E.2.2.1.2

Feel free to modify the **celsius** value to test your program with different temperatures. This exercise helps you become familiar with variables, data types, arithmetic expressions, and the **print()** function with f-strings for formatted output.

Exercise 2.2.2: Calculate the Area and Perimeter of a Rectangle

In this exercise, you will write a Python program that calculates the area and perimeter of a rectangle. You will practice using variables and data types.

Instructions:

1. Create a new Python file or open a Python interpreter.
2. Declare two variables: **length** and **width**. Assign them appropriate values (e.g., 5 and 3, respectively).
3. Calculate the area of the rectangle using the formula **area = length * width**, and assign the result to a variable named **area**.
4. Calculate the perimeter of the rectangle using the formula **perimeter = 2 * (length + width)**, and assign the result to a variable named **perimeter**.
5. Use the **print()** function to display the calculated area and perimeter of the rectangle.

Your final code should look something like this:

```
length = 5
width = 3

area = length * width
perimeter = 2 * (length + width)

print(f"The area of a rectangle with length {length} and width {width} is {area}")
print(f"The perimeter of a rectangle with length {length} and width {width} is {perimeter}")
```

Code block: E.2.2.2.1

When you run your program, you should see output similar to the following:

```
The area of a rectangle with length 5 and width 3 is 15
The perimeter of a rectangle with length 5 and width 3 is 16
```

Code block: E.2.2.2.2

Feel free to modify the **length** and **width** variables to practice with different rectangle dimensions. This exercise helps you become familiar with variables and data types in Python.

Exercise 2.2.3: Simple Interest Calculator

In this exercise, you will write a Python program that calculates the simple interest earned on an investment. You will practice using variables and data types.

Instructions:

1. Create a new Python file or open a Python interpreter.
2. Declare three variables: **principal**, **rate**, and **time**. Assign them appropriate values (e.g., 1000, 0.05, and 3, respectively).
3. Calculate the simple interest using the formula **simple_interest = principal * rate * time**, and assign the result to a variable named **simple_interest**.

4. Use the **print()** function to display the calculated simple interest.

Your final code should look something like this:

```python
principal = 1000
rate = 0.05
time = 3

simple_interest = principal * rate * time

print(f"The simple interest earned on an investment of ${principal} at a rate of {rate * 100}% over {time} years is ${simple_interest}")
```

Code block: E.2.2.3.1

When you run your program, you should see output similar to the following:

```
The simple interest earned on an investment of $1000 at a rate of 5.0% over 3 years is $150.0
```

Code block: E.2.2.3.2

Feel free to modify the variables to practice with different investment scenarios. These exercises help you become familiar with variables and data types in Python.

2.3 Operators

In this section, we will discuss the various operators available in Python. Operators are special symbols that allow you to perform operations on values and variables. Python supports several types of operators, including arithmetic, comparison, assignment, logical, and bitwise operators.

2.3.1 Arithmetic Operators

Arithmetic operators are used to perform basic mathematical operations on values.

- Addition (**+**): Adds two values.
- Subtraction (**``**): Subtracts the right value from the left value.
- Multiplication (**``**): Multiplies two values.
- Division (**/**): Divides the left value by the right value, resulting in a float.
- Floor Division (**//**): Divides the left value by the right value, rounding down to the nearest integer.
- Modulus (**%**): Returns the remainder of the division of the left value by the right value.
- Exponentiation (*****): Raises the left value to the power of the right value.

```python
x = 5
y = 2

print(x + y)   # Output: 7
print(x - y)   # Output: 3
print(x * y)   # Output: 10
print(x / y)   # Output: 2.5
print(x // y)  # Output: 2
print(x % y)   # Output: 1
print(x ** y)  # Output: 25
```

Code block: 2.11

2.3.2 Comparison Operators

Comparison operators are used to compare values and return a boolean result (**True** or **False**).

- Equal to (==): Checks if two values are equal.
- Not equal to (!=): Checks if two values are not equal.
- Greater than (>): Checks if the left value is greater than the right value.
- Less than (<): Checks if the left value is less than the right value.
- Greater than or equal to (>=): Checks if the left value is greater than or equal to the right value.
- Less than or equal to (<=): Checks if the left value is less than or equal to the right value.

```python
x = 5
y = 2

print(x == y)   # Output: False
print(x != y)   # Output: True
print(x > y)    # Output: True
print(x < y)    # Output: False
print(x >= y)   # Output: True
print(x <= y)   # Output: False
```

Code block: 2.12

2.3.3 Assignment Operators

Assignment operators are used to assign values to variables. The basic assignment operator is =, but there are also compound assignment operators that perform an operation and assignment in a single step.

- +=: Adds the right value to the left variable and assigns the result to the left variable.
- =: Subtracts the right value from the left variable and assigns the result to the left variable.
- =: Multiplies the left variable by the right value and assigns the result to the left variable.
- /=: Divides the left variable by the right value and assigns the result to the left variable.
- //=: Performs floor division on the left variable by the right value and assigns the result to the left variable.

- **%=**: Calculates the modulus of the left variable divided by the right value and assigns the result to the left variable.
- ***=**: Raises the left variable to the power of the right value and assigns the result to the left variable.

```
x = 5

x += 3   # Same as x = x + 3, x becomes 8
x -= 2   # Same as x = x - 2, x becomes 6
x *= 4   # Same as x = x * 4, x becomes 24
x /= 3   # Same as x = x / 3, x becomes 8.0
x //= 2  # Same as x = x // 2, x becomes 4.0
x %= 3   # Same as x = x % 3, x becomes 1.0
x **= 2  # Same as x = x ** 2, x becomes 1.0
```

Code block: 2.13

2.3.4 Logical Operator

Logical operators are used to combine boolean expressions and return a boolean result (**True** or **False**).

- **and**: Returns **True** if both expressions are true, otherwise returns **False**.
- **or**: Returns **True** if at least one of the expressions is true, otherwise returns **False**.
- **not**: Returns **True** if the expression is false, and **False** if the expression is true.

```
x = True
y = False

print(x and y)   # Output: False
print(x or y)    # Output: True
print(not x)     # Output: False
```

Code block: 2.14

2.3.5 Bitwise Operators

Bitwise operators perform operations on the binary representation of integers.

- Bitwise AND (&): Performs a bitwise AND operation on two integers.
- Bitwise OR (|): Performs a bitwise OR operation on two integers.
- Bitwise XOR (^): Performs a bitwise XOR operation on two integers.
- Bitwise NOT (~): Inverts the bits of an integer.
- Left Shift (<<): Shifts the bits of an integer to the left by a specified number of positions.
- Right Shift (>>): Shifts the bits of an integer to the right by a specified number of positions.

```python
x = 5  # Binary: 0101
y = 3  # Binary: 0011

print(x & y)   # Output: 1 (Binary: 0001)
print(x | y)   # Output: 7 (Binary: 0111)
print(x ^ y)   # Output: 6 (Binary: 0110)
print(~x)      # Output: -6 (Binary: 1010)
print(x << 2)  # Output: 20 (Binary: 10100)
print(x >> 1)  # Output: 2 (Binary: 0010)
```

Code block: 2.15

Understanding the various operators in Python will enable you to perform complex operations on your data and create more sophisticated programs. As you continue through this book, you will encounter many practical applications of these operators in various programming tasks and challenges.

Exercise 2.3.1: Simple Arithmetic Operations

In this exercise, you will write a Python program that performs basic arithmetic operations (addition, subtraction, multiplication, and division) on two numbers. You will practice using operators and the **print()** function.

Instructions:

1. Create a new Python file or open a Python interpreter.

2. Declare two variables, **num1** and **num2**, and assign them numeric values (e.g., 10 and 5).
3. Calculate the sum, difference, product, and quotient of **num1** and **num2**, and assign the results to the variables **sum**, **difference**, **product**, and **quotient**, respectively.
4. Use the **print()** function to display the results of the arithmetic operations.

Your final code should look something like this:

```python
num1 = 10
num2 = 5

sum = num1 + num2
difference = num1 - num2
product = num1 * num2
quotient = num1 / num2

print(f"Sum: {sum}")
print(f"Difference: {difference}")
print(f"Product: {product}")
print(f"Quotient: {quotient}")
```

Code block: E.2.3.1.1

When you run your program, you should see output similar to the following:

```
Sum: 15
Difference: 5
Product: 50
Quotient: 2.0
```

Code block: E.2.3.1.2

This exercise helps you become familiar with operators and the **print()** function in Python.

Exercise 2.3.2: Maximum of Two Numbers

In this exercise, you will write a Python program that finds the maximum of two numbers entered by the user. You will practice using input, output, and operators.

Instructions:

1. Create a new Python file or open a Python interpreter.
2. Use the **input()** function to prompt the user to enter two numbers, and assign the results to variables **num1** and **num2**. Remember to convert the input to the appropriate data type (e.g., float or int).
3. Use the appropriate operator to find the maximum of the two numbers, and assign the result to a variable named **max_num**.
4. Use the **print()** function to display the maximum of the two numbers.

Your final code should look something like this:

```python
num1 = float(input("Enter the first number: "))
num2 = float(input("Enter the second number: "))

max_num = num1 if num1 > num2 else num2

print(f"The maximum of {num1} and {num2} is {max_num}")
```

Code block: E.2.3.2.1

When you run your program, you should see output similar to the following (depending on user input):

```
Enter the first number: 6.5
Enter the second number: 4.2
The maximum of 6.5 and 4.2 is 6.5
```

Code block: E.2.3.2.2

Exercise 2.3.3: Calculate the Distance Between Two Points

In this exercise, you will write a Python program that calculates the distance between two points in a 2D plane using their coordinates. You will practice using variables, data types, and operators.

Instructions:

1. Create a new Python file or open a Python interpreter.
2. Declare four variables: **x1**, **y1**, **x2**, and **y2**. Assign them appropriate coordinates (e.g., 3, 4, 6, and 8, respectively).
3. Calculate the distance between the two points using the distance formula **distance = ((x2 - x1) ** 2 + (y2 - y1) ** 2) ** 0.5**, and assign the result to a variable named **distance**.
4. Use the **print()** function to display the calculated distance between the two points.

Your final code should look something like this:

```python
x1, y1 = 3, 4
x2, y2 = 6, 8

distance = ((x2 - x1) ** 2 + (y2 - y1) ** 2) ** 0.5

print(f"The distance between point A({x1}, {y1}) and point B({x2}, {y2}) is {distance:.2f}")
```

Code block: E.2.3.3.1

When you run your program, you should see output similar to the following:

```
The distance between point A(3, 4) and point B(6, 8) is 5.00
```

Code block: E.2.3.3.2

Feel free to modify the variables to practice with different coordinates. These exercises help you become familiar with operators in Python.

2.4 Type Conversion

In this section, we will discuss type conversion in Python. Type conversion, also known as type casting, is the process of converting a value from one data type to another. In Python, you can use built-in functions to perform explicit type conversions. It is important to understand how to convert between different data types because certain operations may only work with specific types, or you may need to ensure that your data is in a suitable format for a particular function.

2.4.1 Basic Type Conversion Functions

Here are some of the most commonly used type conversion functions in Python:

- **int()**: Converts a value to an integer. This function can be used to convert floats to integers or numeric strings to integers.
- **float()**: Converts a value to a floating-point number. This function can be used to convert integers to floats or numeric strings to floats.
- **str()**: Converts a value to a string. This function can be used to convert integers, floats, or other types to strings.
- **bool()**: Converts a value to a boolean. This function can be used to convert integers, floats, strings, or other types to boolean values.

Examples of type conversion:

```python
x = 5.5
y = int(x)    # Convert float to int, y becomes 5

a = 3
b = float(a)  # Convert int to float, b becomes 3.0

c = 42
d = str(c)    # Convert int to str, d becomes "42"

e = "123"
f = int(e)    # Convert str to int, f becomes 123

g = "True"
h = bool(g)   # Convert str to bool, h becomes True
```

Code block: 2.16

2.4.2 Type Conversion Limitations

Not all type conversions are valid or possible. For example, if you try to convert a non-numeric string to an integer or a float, a **ValueError** will be raised:

```python
s = "hello"
i = int(s)   # Raises a ValueError: invalid literal for int() with base 10: 'hello'
```

Code block: 2.17

It's important to be aware of the limitations and constraints of type conversions to prevent errors in your code. Always ensure that the value you're trying to convert is compatible with the target data type.

2.4.3 Implicit Type Conversion

Python also performs implicit type conversions, also known as "type coercion," in certain situations. Implicit type conversion occurs when the interpreter automatically converts one data type to another without the programmer explicitly requesting the conversion.

For example, when you perform arithmetic operations between integers and floats, Python automatically converts the integer to a float before performing the operation:

```python
x = 5    # int
y = 2.0  # float

result = x + y   # Python implicitly converts x to a float: 5.0 + 2.0
print(result)    # Output: 7.0
```

Code block: 2.18

In some cases, implicit type conversion can lead to unexpected results or loss of precision, so it's essential to understand how Python handles different data types in various contexts.

Understanding type conversion in Python is crucial for working with different data types and ensuring your data is in the appropriate format. As you progress through this book, you will encounter various situations where type conversion is necessary or useful for solving programming challenges and working with complex data structures.

Exercise 2.4.1: Shopping List Price Calculator

In this exercise, you will write a Python program that calculates the total price of items on a shopping list. You will practice using type conversion, arithmetic operations, and the **print()** function.

Instructions:

1. Create a new Python file or open a Python interpreter.
2. Declare three variables, **item1**, **item2**, and **item3**, representing the prices of three items on the shopping list (e.g., 4.99, 2.75, and 1.25). Use float values for the prices.
3. Calculate the total price by adding the prices of the three items, and assign the result to a variable named **total_price**.
4. Convert the **total_price** to a string, and round the result to two decimal places using the **round()** function. Assign the result to a variable named **formatted_total**.
5. Use the **print()** function to display the total price of the shopping list.

Your final code should look something like this:

```python
item1 = 4.99
item2 = 2.75
item3 = 1.25

total_price = item1 + item2 + item3
formatted_total = round(total_price, 2)

print(f"The total price of the shopping list is ${formatted_total}")
```

Code block: E 2.4.1.1

When you run your program, you should see output similar to the following:

```
The total price of the shopping list is $9.0
```

Code block: E.2.4.1.2

Feel free to modify the item prices to test your program with different shopping list items. This exercise helps you become familiar with type conversion, arithmetic operations, and the **print()** function in Python.

Exercise 2.4.2: Calculate the Average of Three Numbers

In this exercise, you will write a Python program that calculates the average of three numbers entered by the user. You will practice using input, output, type conversion, and arithmetic operators.

Instructions:

1. Create a new Python file or open a Python interpreter.
2. Use the **input()** function to prompt the user to enter three numbers, and assign the results to variables **num1**, **num2**, and **num3**. Remember to convert the input to the appropriate data type (e.g., float or int).
3. Calculate the average of the three numbers using the formula **average = (num1 + num2 + num3) / 3**, and assign the result to a variable named **average**.
4. Use the **print()** function to display the calculated average.

Your final code should look something like this:

```python
num1 = float(input("Enter the first number: "))
num2 = float(input("Enter the second number: "))
num3 = float(input("Enter the third number: "))

average = (num1 + num2 + num3) / 3

print(f"The average of {num1}, {num2}, and {num3} is {average:.2f}")
```

Code block: E.2.4.2.1

When you run your program, you should see output similar to the following (depending on user input):

```
Enter the first number: 4
Enter the second number: 6
Enter the third number: 8
The average of 4.0, 6.0, and 8.0 is 6.00
```

Code block: E.2.4.2.2

Exercise 2.4.3: Convert Seconds to Hours, Minutes, and Seconds

In this exercise, you will write a Python program that converts a given number of seconds into hours, minutes, and seconds. You will practice using variables, type conversion, and arithmetic operators.

Instructions:

1. Create a new Python file or open a Python interpreter.
2. Use the **input()** function to prompt the user to enter a number of seconds, and assign the result to a variable named **total_seconds**. Remember to convert the input to the appropriate data type (e.g., int).
3. Calculate the number of hours, minutes, and remaining seconds using the following formulas:
    - hours = total_seconds // 3600
    - minutes = (total_seconds % 3600) // 60
    - seconds = total_seconds % 60
4. Use the **print()** function to display the result in hours, minutes, and seconds.

Your final code should look something like this:

```
total_seconds = int(input("Enter the number of seconds: "))

hours = total_seconds // 3600
minutes = (total_seconds % 3600) // 60
seconds = total_seconds % 60

print(f"{total_seconds} seconds is equal to {hours} hours, {minutes} minutes, an
d {seconds} seconds.")
```

Code block: E.2.4.3.1

When you run your program, you should see output similar to the following (depending on user input):

```
Enter the number of seconds: 3666
3666 seconds is equal to 1 hours, 1 minutes, and 6 seconds.
```

Code block: E.2.4.3.2

These exercises help you become familiar with type conversion in Python.

2.5 Input and Output

In this section, we will discuss the basic input and output operations in Python. Being able to interact with users and display information is crucial for building interactive applications and presenting the results of your code.

2.5.1 Output: The print() Function

The **print()** function is one of the most commonly used functions in Python for displaying output. It writes text to the console, allowing you to present information to users or debug your code. You can pass one or more arguments to the **print()** function, separated by commas. By default, the **print()** function adds a newline character at the end of the output.

Examples of using the **print()** function:

```
print("Hello, World!")   # Output: Hello, World!

x = 5
y = 3
print("The sum of", x, "and", y, "is", x + y)   # Output: The sum of 5 and 3 is 8
```

Code block: 2.19

You can also customize the **print()** function using its optional parameters, such as **sep** (separator) and **end**. For example:

```
print("A", "B", "C", sep=", ")   # Output: A, B, C
print("Hello", end="! ")          # Output: Hello! (no newline)
```

Code block: 2.20

2.5.2 Input: The input() Function

The **input()** function is used to read user input from the console. It accepts a single optional argument, which is the prompt to be displayed to the user. The function returns the user's input as a string.

Examples of using the **input()** function:

```
name = input("Enter your name: ")
print("Hello, " + name + "!")   # Output: Hello, [user's input]!
```

Code block: 2.21

Since the **input()** function always returns a string, you may need to perform type conversion if you expect a different data type. For example:

```
age_str = input("Enter your age: ")
age = int(age_str)   # Convert the user input to an integer
print("In one year, you will be", age + 1, "years old.")   # Output: In one year, you will be [age+1] years old.
```

Code block: 2.22

2.5.3 Formatting Output: f-strings, str.format(), and %-formatting

Python provides several methods for formatting output strings, making it easier to create well-formatted and readable messages.

- f-strings (Python 3.6 and later): f-strings, or "formatted string literals," allow you to embed expressions and variables directly into string literals, using curly braces {}. To create an f-string, add an **f** or **F** prefix before the string literal.

Example of using f-strings:

```
name = "Alice"
age = 30
print(f"{name} is {age} years old.")   # Output: Alice is 30 years old.
```

Code block: 2.23

- **str.format()**: The **str.format()** method allows you to insert placeholders in a string, which will be replaced by specified values when the method is called. Placeholders are enclosed in curly braces {} and can include optional formatting specifications.

Example of using **str.format()**:

```
name = "Bob"
age = 25
print("{} is {} years old.".format(name, age))   # Output: Bob is 25 years old.
```

Code block: 2.24

- **%-formatting**: The **%** operator can be used for string formatting, similar to the syntax used in C's **printf()** function. This method uses placeholders in the string, which are replaced by specified values. Placeholders begin with a **%** character, followed by a formatting specifier.

Example of using %-formatting:

```
name = "Charlie"
age = 22
print("%s is %d years old." % (name, age))   # Output: Charlie is 22 years old.
```

Code block: 2.25

Some common formatting specifiers include:

- **%s**: String
- **%d**: Integer
- **%f**: Floating-point number

Note that %-formatting is considered less readable and less flexible compared to f-strings and **str.format()**, and it's not recommended for new Python code.

Understanding input and output operations in Python is essential for building interactive applications and presenting the results of your code. As you progress through this book, you will learn more advanced techniques for formatting output, handling files, and working with data streams to create more complex and versatile applications.

Exercise 2.5.1: Personalized Greeting

In this exercise, you will write a Python program that prompts the user for their name and age, and then displays a personalized greeting. You will practice using input, output, and type conversion.

Instructions:

1. Create a new Python file or open a Python interpreter.
2. Use the **input()** function to prompt the user to enter their name, and assign the result to a variable named **name**.
3. Use the **input()** function again to prompt the user to enter their age. Remember to convert the input to the appropriate data type (e.g., int), and assign the result to a variable named **age**.
4. Calculate the year the user was born using the current year minus the user's age, and assign the result to a variable named **birth_year**.
5. Use the **print()** function to display a personalized greeting, including the user's name and birth year.

Your final code should look something like this:

```python
name = input("Enter your name: ")
age = int(input("Enter your age: "))

current_year = 2023  # Replace with the current year
birth_year = current_year - age

print(f"Hello, {name}! You were born in {birth_year}.")
```

Code block: E.2.5.1.1

When you run your program, you should see output similar to the following (depending on user input):

```
Enter your name: Jane
Enter your age: 25
Hello, Jane! You were born in 1998.
```

Code block: E.2.5.1.2

Exercise 2.5.2: Personal Information Form

In this exercise, you will write a Python program that prompts the user to enter their personal information and then displays it. You will practice using input, output, and string formatting.

Instructions:

1. Create a new Python file or open a Python interpreter.
2. Use the **input()** function to prompt the user to enter their first name, last name, age, and email address. Assign the results to variables **first_name**, **last_name**, **age**, and **email**.
3. Use the **print()** function and string formatting to display the entered information in a user-friendly format.

Your final code should look something like this:

```python
first_name = input("Enter your first name: ")
last_name = input("Enter your last name: ")
age = input("Enter your age: ")
email = input("Enter your email address: ")

print(f"Name: {first_name} {last_name}\nAge: {age}\nEmail: {email}")
```

Code block: E.2.5.2.1

When you run your program, you should see output similar to the following (depending on user input):

```
Enter your first name: John
Enter your last name: Doe
Enter your age: 30
Enter your email address: john.doe@example.com
Name: John Doe
Age: 30
Email: john.doe@example.com
```

Code block: E.2.5.2.2

Exercise 2.5.3: Calculate the Area and Circumference of a Circle

In this exercise, you will write a Python program that calculates the area and circumference of a circle using its radius. You will practice using input, output, variables, arithmetic operators, and the **math** module.

Instructions:

1. Create a new Python file or open a Python interpreter.
2. Import the **math** module by adding **import math** at the beginning of your code.
3. Use the **input()** function to prompt the user to enter the radius of a circle, and assign the result to a variable named **radius**. Remember to convert the input to the appropriate data type (e.g., float).
4. Calculate the area and circumference of the circle using the following formulas:
    - area = math.pi * radius ** 2
    - circumference = 2 * math.pi * radius
5. Use the **print()** function to display the calculated area and circumference of the circle.

Your final code should look something like this:

```python
import math

radius = float(input("Enter the radius of the circle: "))

area = math.pi * radius ** 2
circumference = 2 * math.pi * radius

print(f"The area of a circle with radius {radius} is {area:.2f}")
print(f"The circumference of a circle with radius {radius} is {circumference:.2f}")
```

Code block: E.2.5.3.1

When you run your program, you should see output similar to the following (depending on user input):

```
Enter the radius of the circle: 5
The area of a circle with radius 5.0 is 78.54
The circumference of a circle with radius 5.0 is 31.42
```

Code block: E.2.5.3.2

CHAPTER 3: Data Structures

Welcome to Chapter 3, "Data Structures." In this chapter, we will explore some of the most widely used data structures in Python, such as lists, tuples, sets, and dictionaries. Understanding these data structures is crucial for organizing, processing, and storing data efficiently in your Python programs.

Python provides a variety of data structures that can be used to store different types of data, such as integers, strings, and even other data structures. Lists, for instance, are a type of sequence data structure that can be used to store a collection of values, such as the names of students in a class or the temperatures recorded in a weather station. Tuples, on the other hand, are similar to lists, but they are immutable, meaning that their values cannot be changed once they are defined. Sets are another type of data structure that can be used to store a collection of unique values, while dictionaries are a type of data structure that can be used to store key-value pairs, such as the names and ages of people in a database.

By learning about these data structures, you will be able to write more efficient and effective Python code, as well as understand how popular Python libraries, such as Pandas and NumPy, use these data structures to manipulate large amounts of data. So, let's dive in and explore the fascinating world of data structures in Python!

3.1: Lists

Python's list is a powerful data structure that allows for the creation of mutable, ordered collections of items. Lists are incredibly versatile and can contain elements of any type, including numbers, strings, other lists, or even custom objects. Moreover, lists are the foundation for many complex data structures and algorithms in Python, making them essential for programming in this language.

For instance, lists can be used to store and manipulate data in a variety of ways. One of the most common uses of lists is to represent sequences of data, such as a list of numbers or strings. In addition, lists can be used to hold items of different types or even other lists, which makes them particularly useful in situations where data needs to be grouped together. Because lists are mutable, it is possible to add, remove, or modify elements as needed, which makes them ideal for dynamic data structures.

Furthermore, lists can be sorted, sliced, and concatenated, allowing for a wide range of operations to be performed on them. For example, the sorted() function can be used to sort the elements of a list in ascending or descending order, while slicing can be used to extract a subset of the list. Additionally, lists can be concatenated using the + operator, which allows two or more lists to be combined into a single list.

Overall, Python's list is a fundamental data structure that plays an important role in many aspects of programming. Its versatility and flexibility make it indispensable for working with data in Python, making it an essential skill for any programmer to master.

To create a list, you can simply place a comma-separated sequence of elements inside square brackets:

```
my_list = [1, 2, 3, "hello", 4.5]
```

Code block: 3.1

You can access individual elements of a list using their index, starting with zero for the first element:

```
first_element = my_list[0]    # 1
second_element = my_list[1]   # 2
```

Code block: 3.2

Lists support various operations, such as adding or removing elements, slicing, and modifying elements in place:

```python
# Adding an element to the end of the list
my_list.append(6)

# Removing an element by its index
del my_list[3]

# Slicing a list
sub_list = my_list[1:4]

# Modifying an element in place
my_list[2] = 42
```

Code block: 3.3

Python also provides several built-in functions to manipulate lists, like **len()** to get the length of a list, **sorted()** to return a sorted version of the list, and **sum()** to calculate the sum of the list elements (if they are numeric).

```python
list_length = len(my_list)
sorted_list = sorted(my_list)
list_sum = sum(my_list)
```

Code block: 3.4

In the upcoming sections of this chapter, we will expand our understanding of additional data structures and how they can be utilized. Along with exploring these concepts in greater depth, we will provide you with a comprehensive array of detailed explanations and practical exercises, all designed to further develop your skills and provide you with hands-on experience working with Python's data structures.

By the time you have completed this chapter, you will have a thorough understanding of these concepts and how to apply them to real-world situations.

Exercise 3.1.1: Creating and Accessing Lists

In this exercise, you will create a list and access its elements using indices.

Instructions:

1. Create a list containing the integers from 1 to 5.
2. Print the first, third, and fifth elements of the list.

Solution:

```
my_list = [1, 2, 3, 4, 5]
print(my_list[0], my_list[2], my_list[4])
```

Code block: E.3.1.1.1

Output:

```
1 3 5
```

Code block: E.3.1.1.2

Exercise 3.1.2: List Manipulation

In this exercise, you will perform various operations on a list, such as adding, removing, and modifying elements.

Instructions:

1. Create a list with the elements **["apple", "banana", "cherry"]**.
2. Add the element "orange" to the end of the list.
3. Remove the element "banana" from the list.
4. Replace the element "cherry" with "grape".
5. Print the modified list.

Solution Code:

```python
fruits = ["apple", "banana", "cherry"]
fruits.append("orange")
fruits.remove("banana")
fruits[1] = "grape"
print(fruits)
```

Code block: E.3.1.2.1

Output:

```
['apple', 'grape', 'orange']
```

Code block: E.3.1.2.2

Exercise 3.1.3: List Slicing

In this exercise, you will use slicing to extract a sublist from a given list.

Instructions:

1. Create a list with the elements **[1, 2, 3, 4, 5, 6, 7, 8, 9]**.
2. Extract a sublist containing the elements from index 3 (inclusive) to index 7 (exclusive).
3. Print the extracted sublist.

Solution:

```python
numbers = [1, 2, 3, 4, 5, 6, 7, 8, 9]
sublist = numbers[3:7]
print(sublist)
```

Code block: E.3.1.3.1

Output:

```
(4, 5, 6, 7)
```

Code block. E.3.1.3.2

3.2: Tuples

In this section, we will explore the concept of tuples, which are a type of built-in data structure in Python. Similar to lists, tuples are used to store collections of related values. However, unlike lists, tuples are immutable, meaning that once they are created, their elements cannot be modified. This property makes tuples useful for situations where you need to ensure that the data you are working with remains static throughout the execution of your program.

One common use case for tuples is when you need to store a set of values that are related to each other, such as a person's name, age, and address. By grouping these values together in a tuple, you can ensure that they remain associated with each other throughout your program's execution. Additionally, because tuples are immutable, you can be confident that the data you are working with will not be inadvertently modified, which can help to avoid bugs and other issues in your code.

Another advantage of tuples is that they can be used as keys in dictionaries, which are another important data structure in Python. Because tuples are immutable, they can be safely used as dictionary keys, whereas lists cannot. This makes tuples a valuable tool for working with dictionaries and other data structures that rely on key-value pairs.

Overall, tuples are a powerful and versatile tool in Python that can help you to efficiently store and manage related data in your programs. Whether you are working on a small script or a large-scale application, understanding how to use tuples effectively can help you to write cleaner, more efficient code that is less prone to errors and bugs.

3.2.1: Creating Tuples:

To create a tuple, use parentheses and separate the elements with commas:

```
my_tuple = (1, 2, 3)
```

Code block: 3.5

You can also create a tuple without parentheses, just by separating the elements with commas:

```
my_tuple = 1, 2, 3
```

Code block: 3.6

A tuple with a single element should have a trailing comma:

```
single_element_tuple = (4,)
```

Code block: 3.7

3.2.2: Accessing Tuple Elements:

To access elements in a tuple, use indexing, just like you would with a list:

```
my_tuple = (1, 2, 3)
print(my_tuple[0])   # Output: 1
print(my_tuple[1])   # Output: 2
print(my_tuple[2])   # Output: 3
```

Code block: 3.8

Remember that tuple indices start at 0, just like list indices.

3.2.3: Tuple Unpacking:

You can use tuple unpacking to assign the elements of a tuple to multiple variables:

```python
my_tuple = (1, 2, 3)
a, b, c = my_tuple
print(a)  # Output: 1
print(b)  # Output: 2
print(c)  # Output: 3
```

Code block: 3.9

3.2.4: Immutability:

As mentioned earlier, tuples are immutable. If you try to modify a tuple, you'll get a TypeError:

```python
my_tuple = (1, 2, 3)
my_tuple[1] = 4  # Raises a TypeError
```

Code block: 3.10

You can, however, create a new tuple by concatenating two existing tuples:

```python
tuple1 = (1, 2, 3)
tuple2 = (4, 5, 6)
new_tuple = tuple1 + tuple2
print(new_tuple)  # Output: (1, 2, 3, 4, 5, 6)
```

Code block: 3.11

In conclusion, tuples are a highly useful data structure when you need an immutable collection of related values. Tuples are often the preferred choice when you need to ensure that the values within them remain constant, as they are not modifiable once created.

Furthermore, tuples can be used in a wide variety of situations where you might normally use a list. For example, a tuple can be used to represent a fixed set of values, such as the x and y coordinates of a point on a graph.

Additionally, tuples can be used to return multiple values from a function. This makes tuples a powerful tool for programming in Python, as they allow you to pass multiple values between functions with ease.

So, while tuples may seem like a relatively simple data structure at first glance, they are actually quite powerful and versatile. Whether you're working with data that needs to remain constant or simply need a way to pass multiple values between functions, tuples are an excellent choice.

Exercise 3.2.1: Creating Tuples

In this exercise, you will create tuples to store information about different fruits.

Instructions:

1. Create a tuple named **apple** that contains the strings "red" and "sweet".
2. Create a tuple named **banana** that contains the strings "yellow" and "sweet".
3. Create a tuple named **lemon** that contains the strings "yellow" and "sour".
4. Print all three tuples.

Solution:

```python
apple = ("red", "sweet")
banana = ("yellow", "sweet")
lemon = ("yellow", "sour")

print(apple)
print(banana)
print(lemon)
```

Code block: 3.2.1.1

Output:

```
('red', 'sweet')
('yellow', 'sweet')
('yellow', 'sour')
```

Code block: 3.2.1.2

Exercise 3.2.2: Accessing Tuple Elements

In this exercise, you will access and print specific elements from a tuple.

Instructions:

1. Create a tuple named **colors** with the following elements: "red", "blue", "green", "yellow", "purple".
2. Print the first, third, and last elements of the tuple.

Solution:

```
colors = ("red", "blue", "green", "yellow", "purple")

print(colors[0])
print(colors[2])
print(colors[-1])
```

Code block: 3.2.2.1

Output:

```
red
green
purple
```

Code block: 3.2.2.2

Exercise 3.2.3: Tuple Unpacking

In this exercise, you will use tuple unpacking to assign individual tuple elements to separate variables.

Instructions:

1. Create a tuple named **coordinates** with the following elements: 35.6895, 139.6917.
2. Use tuple unpacking to assign the tuple elements to two variables named **latitude** and **longitude**.
3. Print the **latitude** and **longitude** variables.

Solution:

```python
coordinates = (35.6895, 139.6917)

latitude, longitude = coordinates

print(latitude)
print(longitude)
```

Code block: 3.2.3.1

Output:

```
35.6895
139.6917
```

Code block: 3.2.3.2

3.3: Sets

A set is a collection data type in Python that is both unordered and unindexed. In other words, sets do not have any particular order and cannot be accessed by index. What's interesting about sets is that they store unique elements, which means that they do not allow duplicate values. This feature makes them particularly useful for certain tasks, such as removing duplicates from a list or performing mathematical set operations like union, intersection, and difference.

Additionally, sets can be modified by adding or removing elements, which can be done using built-in methods like add() and remove(). In short, sets are a powerful tool in Python that can help streamline your code and make it more efficient by allowing you to work with unique elements in a flexible and intuitive way.

3.3.1: Creating a Set:

To create a set, you can use curly braces **{}** and separate the elements with commas or use the built-in **set()** function. Remember that sets cannot have duplicate values.

Example:

```python
my_set = {1, 2, 3, 4}
print(my_set)

# Creating a set using the set() function
my_set2 = set([1, 2, 3, 4])
print(my_set2)
```

Code block: 3.12

Output:

```
{1, 2, 3, 4}
{1, 2, 3, 4}
```

Code block: 3.13

3.3.2: Adding and Removing Elements:

To add an element to a set, you can use the **add()** method. To remove an element, you can use the **remove()** or **discard()** methods. The **remove()** method raises a KeyError if the element is not found, whereas the **discard()** method does not raise any error.

Example:

```python
my_set = {1, 2, 3, 4}

# Add an element to the set
my_set.add(5)
print(my_set)

# Remove an element from the set
my_set.remove(5)
print(my_set)

# Discard an element from the set
my_set.discard(4)
print(my_set)
```

Code block: 3.14

Output:

```
{1, 2, 3, 4, 5}
{1, 2, 3, 4}
{1, 2, 3}
```

Code block: 3.15

3.3.3: Set Operations:

You can perform mathematical set operations like union, intersection, and difference using Python's set methods or operators.

Example:

```python
set1 = {1, 2, 3, 4}
set2 = {3, 4, 5, 6}

# Union of two sets
print(set1.union(set2))    # Using the union() method
print(set1 | set2)         # Using the '|' operator

# Intersection of two sets
print(set1.intersection(set2))   # Using the intersection() method
print(set1 & set2)               # Using the '&' operator

# Difference of two sets
print(set1.difference(set2))   # Using the difference() method
print(set1 - set2)             # Using the '-' operator
```

Code block: 3.16

Output:

```
{1, 2, 3, 4, 5, 6}
{1, 2, 3, 4, 5, 6}
{3, 4}
{3, 4}
{1, 2}
{1, 2}
```

Code block: 3.17

In this section, you've learned about sets in Python, including what they are and how to create them. Sets are a data structure that allow you to store a collection of unique values. You also learned how to add and remove elements from a set, as well as perform various set operations such as union, intersection, and difference.

Sets are a powerful tool for dealing with unique values and performing mathematical operations on collections. They can be used to remove duplicates from a list, find common elements between multiple lists, and much more. In addition, sets are very efficient when it comes to membership testing, making them a good choice when dealing with large collections of data.

Overall, sets are a valuable tool to have in your Python toolkit, and can help you solve many different types of problems.

Exercise 3.3.1: Creating and Modifying Sets

In this exercise, you will create and modify sets to store unique elements.

Instructions:

1. Create a set named **fruits** containing the strings "apple", "banana", "orange", "grape".
2. Add "mango" to the set.
3. Remove "grape" from the set.
4. Print the **fruits** set.

Solution:

```python
fruits = {"apple", "banana", "orange", "grape"}

fruits.add("mango")
fruits.remove("grape")

print(fruits)
```

Code block: E.3.3.1.1

Output:

```
{'orange', 'apple', 'mango', 'banana'}
```

Code block: E.3.3.1.2

Note: The order of elements in the output may vary.

Exercise 3.3.2: Set Operations

In this exercise, you will perform set operations like union and intersection.

Instructions:

1. Create a set named **set1** containing the numbers 1, 2, 3, and 4.
2. Create a set named **set2** containing the numbers 3, 4, 5, and 6.
3. Find the union of **set1** and **set2** and print the result.
4. Find the intersection of **set1** and **set2** and print the result.

Solution:

```python
set1 = {1, 2, 3, 4}
set2 = {3, 4, 5, 6}

union_result = set1.union(set2)
intersection_result = set1.intersection(set2)

print(union_result)
print(intersection_result)
```

Code block: E.3.3.2.1

Output:

```
{1, 2, 3, 4, 5, 6}
{3, 4}
```

Code block: E.3.3.2.2

Exercise 3.3.3: Set Comprehension

In this exercise, you will use set comprehension to create a set of unique elements that meet a specific condition.

Instructions:

1. Create a list named **numbers** containing the numbers 1, 2, 3, 2, 4, 3, 5, 6, 5.
2. Use set comprehension to create a set named **even_numbers** containing the unique even numbers from the **numbers** list.
3. Print the **even_numbers** set.

Solution:

```
numbers = [1, 2, 3, 2, 4, 3, 5, 6, 5]

even_numbers = {num for num in numbers if num % 2 == 0}

print(even_numbers)
```

Code block: E.3.3.3.1

Output:

```
{2, 4, 6}
```

Code block: E.3.3.3.2

3.4: Dictionaries

In this section, we will explore dictionaries, another important data structure in Python. Dictionaries are a powerful tool for storing and organizing data. They are unordered, which means that the elements are not stored in any particular order. They are also mutable, which means that you can add, remove, or modify elements as needed. Dictionaries store key-value pairs, which means that each element in the dictionary is accessed by a unique key. This makes dictionaries useful when you need to store and retrieve data based on a specific identifier or key.

In addition, dictionaries are often used in conjunction with other data structures, such as lists or sets, to create complex data structures that can be used for a wide range of applications. Overall, dictionaries are an essential tool for any Python developer who needs to work with large amounts of data in an efficient and organized manner.

To create a dictionary, you can use curly braces {} and separate the keys and values with colons. Here's an example:

```python
person = {
    "name": "John",
    "age": 30,
    "city": "New York"
}
```

Code block: 3.18

In this example, the keys are **"name"**, **"age"**, and **"city"**, and their corresponding values are **"John"**, 30, and **"New York"**.

Accessing values: To access the value associated with a key, use the key inside square brackets **[ ]**:

```
name = person["name"]
print(name)    # Output: John
```

Code block: 3.19

Adding and updating key-value pairs: To add a new key-value pair or update an existing one, use the key inside square brackets **[ ]** and assign the value using the **=** operator:

```
person["country"] = "USA"          # Adds a new key-value pair
person["city"] = "San Francisco"   # Updates the value for the "city" key
```

Code block: 3.20

Deleting key-value pairs: To remove a key-value pair from the dictionary, use the **del** keyword followed by the key in square brackets **[ ]**:

```
del person["age"]
```

Code block: 3.21

Methods for dictionaries: Python provides several built-in methods for working with dictionaries, such as **keys()**, **values()**, and **items()**. These methods return views of the dictionary's keys, values, and key-value pairs, respectively:

```
keys = person.keys()
values = person.values()
items = person.items()
```

Code block: 3.22

Iterating over a dictionary: You can iterate over a dictionary using a **for** loop. By default, iterating over a dictionary iterates over its keys:

```
for key in person:
    print(key, person[key])
```

Code block: 3.23

Alternatively, you can use the **items()** method to iterate over both keys and values:

```
for key, value in person.items():
    print(key, value)
```

Code block: 3.24

Dictionary comprehension: Like with lists and sets, you can also use dictionary comprehensions to create dictionaries in a concise way. Here's an example:

```
squares = {x: x * x for x in range(1, 6)}
print(squares)  # Output: {1: 1, 2: 4, 3: 9, 4: 16, 5: 25}
```

Code block: 3.25

In this section, we've covered the basics of dictionaries in Python. Dictionaries are a useful data structure that allow us to store key-value pairs. This means that we can associate a value with a specific key, making it easy to lookup values based on their corresponding keys.

We discussed how to create dictionaries in Python using curly braces or the dict() function, and how to access values by using the corresponding key. Additionally, we explored how to add and update key-value pairs in a dictionary using assignment, and how to delete key-value pairs using the del keyword. Finally, we learned how to iterate over dictionaries using loops, which allows us to access all the keys or values in a dictionary.

Exercise 3.4.1: Create a Dictionary

In this exercise, you'll create a dictionary to store information about a movie.

Instructions:

1. Create a dictionary called **movie** with the following keys and values:
    - "title" with the value "Inception"
    - "director" with the value "Christopher Nolan"
    - "year" with the value 2010
    - "rating" with the value 8.8
2. Print the dictionary.

Solution:

```python
movie = {
    "title": "Inception",
    "director": "Christopher Nolan",
    "year": 2010,
    "rating": 8.8
}

print(movie)
```

Code block: E.3.4.1.1

Output:

```
{'title': 'Inception', 'director': 'Christopher Nolan', 'year': 2010, 'rating': 8.8}
```

Code block: E.3.4.1.2

Exercise 3.4.2: Accessing and Modifying Dictionary Values

In this exercise, you'll access and modify the values in a dictionary.

Instructions:

1. Using the **movie** dictionary from the previous exercise, print the movie's title.
2. Update the movie's rating to 9.0.
3. Print the updated dictionary.

Solution:

```python
print(movie["title"])

movie["rating"] = 9.0

print(movie)
```

Code block: E.3.4.2.1

Output:

```
Inception
{'title': 'Inception', 'director': 'Christopher Nolan', 'year': 2010, 'rating': 9.0}
```

Code block: E.3.4.2.2

Exercise 3.4.3: Iterating Over a Dictionary

In this exercise, you'll iterate over the key-value pairs in a dictionary.

Instructions:

1. Using the **movie** dictionary from the previous exercise, iterate over its key-value pairs.
2. Print each key-value pair in the format "key: value".

Solution:

```python
for key, value in movie.items():
    print(f"{key}: {value}")
```

Code block: E.3.4.3.1

Output:

```
title: Inception
director: Christopher Nolan
year: 2010
rating: 9.0
```

Code block: E.3.4.3.2

In conclusion, Chapter 3 introduced you to some of the most commonly used data structures in Python: lists, tuples, sets, and dictionaries. These data structures are essential tools in a programmer's toolbox and can be used to organize, store, and manipulate data efficiently.

Throughout this chapter, you learned how to create and manipulate these data structures, perform common operations such as adding, removing, and updating elements, and iterate through their contents. Each data structure has unique properties and use cases, so understanding their differences and selecting the right one for a particular problem is crucial.

By completing the exercises provided in this chapter, you have gained hands-on experience in working with these data structures. As you continue your journey in Python programming, you will find that your understanding of these data structures will enable you to tackle more complex problems and build more sophisticated applications. Keep practicing and experimenting with different scenarios to further solidify your knowledge and skills.

With the foundation of data structures in place, you are now better prepared to explore more advanced topics and techniques in Python. Keep up the great work, and see you next chapter!

Chapter 4: Control Structures

In this chapter, we will delve into the numerous control structures available in Python, which allow you to create more complex and dynamic programs. Control structures are the backbone of any programming language, as they enable you to control the flow of your program's execution based on conditions or loops.

First, we will cover conditional statements, which allow your program to make decisions based on certain conditions. These statements include if, elif, and else statements, which are used to execute different blocks of code depending on the outcome of the condition.

Next, we will move on to loops, which are used to execute a block of code repeatedly. There are two main types of loops in Python: for loops and while loops. For loops are used to iterate over a sequence of elements, while loops are used to execute a block of code repeatedly as long as a certain condition is true.

Finally, we will explore the use of break and continue statements, which allow you to modify the behavior of your loops. The break statement is used to exit a loop prematurely, while the continue statement is used to skip over certain iterations of a loop.

Overall, understanding control structures is essential for any Python programmer looking to create more advanced programs, and this chapter will equip you with the knowledge needed to do just that.

4.1: Conditional Statements (if, elif, else)

In Python, conditional statements are used to make decisions based on certain conditions. These statements help you to control the flow of your program, allowing it to react differently depending on the input or the current state of your data. The primary conditional statements in Python are **if**, **elif**, and **else**.

The **if** statement is used to test a condition. If the condition is true, the code block following the **if** statement will be executed. The general syntax of an **if** statement is as follows:

```
if condition:
    # Code to be executed if the condition is true
```

Code block: 4.1

For example, let's say we want to check if a number is positive:

```
number = 5

if number > 0:
    print("The number is positive.")
```

Code block: 4.2

The **elif** (short for "else if") statement is used when you want to test multiple conditions. It is placed after an **if** statement and is executed only if the previous conditions were false. The general syntax of an **elif** statement is as follows:

```
if condition1:
    # Code to be executed if condition1 is true
elif condition2:
    # Code to be executed if condition1 is false and condition2 is true
```

Code block: 4.3

For example, let's say we want to check if a number is positive, negative, or zero:

```python
number = 0

if number > 0:
    print("The number is positive.")
elif number < 0:
    print("The number is negative.")
```

Code block: 4.3

The **else** statement is used to execute code when none of the previous conditions are met (i.e., they are all false). It is placed after the **if** and/or **elif** statements. The general syntax of an **else** statement is as follows:

```python
if condition1:
    # Code to be executed if condition1 is true
elif condition2:
    # Code to be executed if condition1 is false and condition2 is true
else:
    # Code to be executed if all conditions are false
```

Code block: 4.4

Continuing with the previous example, let's add an **else** statement to handle the case when the number is zero:

```python
number = 0

if number > 0:
    print("The number is positive.")
elif number < 0:
    print("The number is negative.")
else:
    print("The number is zero.")
```

Code block: 4.5

In summary, conditional statements in Python are a fundamental programming concept that allow you to control the flow of your program based on specific conditions. By using **if**, **elif**, and **else** statements, you can execute different code blocks depending on the given conditions. This is a powerful tool that you can use to create complex programs with dynamic behavior.

Moreover, mastering control structures is essential for any programmer. Beyond conditional statements, loops are another important control structure that you will encounter frequently. With loops, you can iterate through a set of instructions repeatedly until a certain condition is met. This can be useful for tasks such as data processing or user input validation.

Another advanced control structure is the use of **break** and **continue** statements. These statements allow you to modify the behavior of loops based on certain conditions. For example, you can use a **break** statement to terminate a loop early if a specific condition is met. On the other hand, a **continue** statement can be used to skip over a certain iteration of the loop if a condition is met.

In the following topics, we will discuss these and other control structures in more detail, so that you can become a more proficient Python programmer.

Exercise 4.1.1: Odd or Even Number

In this exercise, you will write a Python program that determines if a given number is odd or even. You will practice using **if** and **else** statements.

Instructions:

1. Create a new Python file or open a Python interpreter.
2. Assign an integer value to a variable named **number**.
3. Use an **if** statement to check if the number is even (i.e., divisible by 2) and print a message indicating that it's an even number.
4. Use an **else** statement to handle the case where the number is odd and print a message indicating that it's an odd number.

Your final code should look something like this:

```
number = 7

if number % 2 == 0:
    print(f"{number} is an even number.")
else:
    print(f"{number} is an odd number.")
```

Code blok: E.4.1.1.1

Output example:

```
7 is an odd number.
```

Code blok: E.4.1.1.2

Exercise 4.1.2: Age Group Classification

In this exercise, you will write a Python program that classifies a person's age group based on their age. You will practice using **if**, **elif**, and **else** statements.

Instructions:

1. Create a new Python file or open a Python interpreter.
2. Assign an integer value to a variable named **age**.
3. Use **if**, **elif**, and **else** statements to classify the age group as "Child" (0-12), "Teenager" (13-19), "Adult" (20-59), or "Senior" (60 and above), and print the corresponding classification.

Your final code should look something like this:

```
age = 25

if age >= 0 and age <= 12:
    print("Child")
elif age >= 13 and age <= 19:
    print("Teenager")
elif age >= 20 and age <= 59:
    print("Adult")
else:
    print("Senior")
```

Code blok E.4.1.2.1

Output example:

```
Adult
```

Code blok. E.4.1.2.2

Exercise 4.1.3: Letter Grade Calculation

In this exercise, you will write a Python program that assigns a letter grade based on a student's test score. You will practice using **if**, **elif**, and **else** statements.

Instructions:

1. Create a new Python file or open a Python interpreter.
2. Assign an integer value (0-100) to a variable named **score**.
3. Use **if**, **elif**, and **else** statements to assign a letter grade (A, B, C, D, or F) based on the score, and print the corresponding letter grade.

The grading scale is as follows:

- A: 90-100

- B: 80-89
- C: 70-79
- D: 60-69
- F: 0-59

Your final code should look something like this:

```python
score = 85

if score >= 90 and score <= 100:
    print("A")
elif score >= 80 and score < 90:
    print("B")
elif score >= 70 and score < 80:
    print("C")
elif score >= 60 and score < 70:
    print("D")
else:
    print("F")
```

Code blok: E.4.1.3.1

Output example:

```
B
```

Code blok: E.4.1.3.2

These exercises help you become familiar with using conditional statements in Python to control the flow of your programs.

4.2: Loops (for, while)

Loops are an essential control structure in Python as they provide the ability to repeat a block of code multiple times, based on certain conditions or a specified range. By using loops, you can perform repetitive tasks, such as iterating through a list or executing a block of code a specific number of times.

In this topic, we will explore two types of loops available in Python: **for** loops and **while** loops. A **for** loop is used to iterate over a sequence, such as a list, tuple, or string. The **for** loop executes the block of code inside it for each item in the sequence. On the other hand, a **while** loop is used to execute a block of code repeatedly as long as a certain condition is met.

for loops and **while** loops can be nested within each other, which means that you can have a loop inside another loop. This can be useful when you need to iterate over multiple sequences or perform a repetitive task with a changing condition.

Loops are an essential component of Python programming as they provide a way to perform repetitive tasks efficiently. By understanding the different types of loops and their syntax, you can write more complex programs that perform a variety of tasks.

4.2.1 for Loop:

A **for** loop is used to iterate over a sequence, such as a list, tuple, string, or any other iterable object. It executes the block of code for each item in the sequence. The general syntax of a **for** loop is as follows:

```python
for variable in sequence:
    # Code to be executed for each item in the sequence
```

Code block: 4.6

For example, let's say we want to iterate through a list of numbers and print each number:

```
numbers = [1, 2, 3, 4, 5]

for number in numbers:
    print(number)
```

Code block: 4.7

Output:

```
1
2
3
4
5
```

Code block: 4.8

4.2.2 range() Function:

The **range()** function is commonly used with **for** loops when you want to iterate over a range of numbers. The function generates a sequence of numbers starting from 0 (by default) and up to (but not including) the specified number. The syntax for the **range()** function is:

```
range(stop)
```

Code block: 4.9

You can also specify a starting number and a step value as optional arguments:

```
range(start, stop[, step])
```

Code block: 4.10

For example, let's say we want to print the numbers from 0 to 4:

```
for i in range(5):
    print(i)
```

Code block: 4.11

Output:

```
0
1
2
3
4
```

Code block: 4.11

4.2.3 while Loop:

A **while** loop is used to repeatedly execute a block of code as long as a given condition is true. The general syntax of a **while** loop is as follows:

```
while condition:
    # Code to be executed while the condition is true
```

Code block: 4.12

For example, let's say we want to print the numbers from 1 to 5 using a **while** loop:

```python
number = 1

while number <= 5:
    print(number)
    number += 1
```

Code block: 4.13

Output:

```
1
2
3
4
5
```

Code block: 4.14

In summary, loops are an essential aspect of Python because they allow you to execute a block of code multiple times based on specific conditions or ranges. This makes it easier to automate repetitive tasks and code with fewer lines. Using **for** loops, you can iterate over sequences, such as lists or tuples, and perform operations on each element. This is useful for tasks such as summing or filtering items in a list. On the other hand, **while** loops enable you to execute code as long as a given condition is true. This is useful for repetitive tasks or situations where you don't know how many times you need to execute the code.

In the following topics, we will delve deeper into the use of break and continue statements in loops. A **break** statement allows you to exit a loop prematurely, while a **continue** statement skips over the current iteration and jumps to the next one. These statements can be used to control the behavior of loops and make them more efficient. We will also discuss nested loops, which involve using one loop inside another. Nested loops are commonly used in tasks such as matrix multiplication or searching through a list of lists. Finally, we will cover loop control techniques, such as using counters or flags to control the flow of execution in a loop. These techniques can make your code more readable and easier to maintain.

Exercise 4.2.1: Sum of Numbers

In this exercise, you will write a Python program that calculates the sum of all numbers from 1 to a given number (inclusive) using a **for** loop.

Instructions:

1. Create a new Python file or open a Python interpreter.
2. Assign an integer value to a variable named **n**.
3. Use a **for** loop and the **range()** function to iterate through the numbers from 1 to **n** (inclusive).
4. Calculate the sum of the numbers and store it in a variable named **total**.
5. Print the value of **total** after the loop is complete.

Your final code should look something like this:

```python
n = 10
total = 0

for i in range(1, n + 1):
    total += i

print(total)
```

Code block: E.4.2.1.1

Output:

```
55
```

Code block: E.4.2.1.2

Exercise 4.2.2: Reverse a String

In this exercise, you will write a Python program that reverses a given string using a **for** loop.

Instructions:

1. Create a new Python file or open a Python interpreter.
2. Assign a string value to a variable named **text**.
3. Use a **for** loop to iterate through the characters in the string in reverse order.
4. Append each character to a new string named **reversed_text**.
5. Print the value of **reversed_text** after the loop is complete.

Your final code should look something like this:

```python
text = "Python"
reversed_text = ""

for char in reversed(text):
    reversed_text += char

print(reversed_text)
```

Code block: E.4.2.2.1

Output:

```
nohtyP
```

Code block: E.4.2.2.2

Exercise 4.2.3: Countdown Timer

In this exercise, you will write a Python program that acts as a countdown timer using a **while** loop.

Instructions:

1. Create a new Python file or open a Python interpreter.
2. Assign an integer value to a variable named **countdown**.
3. Use a **while** loop to count down from the given number to 0 (inclusive).
4. Print the current value of the countdown in each iteration.
5. Use the **time.sleep()** function from the **time** module to pause the program for 1 second between each countdown step.

Your final code should look something like this:

```python
import time

countdown = 5

while countdown >= 0:
    print(countdown)
    time.sleep(1)
    countdown -= 1

print("Time's up!")
```

Code block: E.4.2.3.1

Output:

```
5
4
3
2
1
0
Time's up!
```

Code block: E.4.2.3.2

These exercises help you practice using **for** and **while** loops in Python to control the flow of your programs and accomplish various tasks.

4.3: Loop Control (break, continue)

When working with loops, there may be situations where you need more control over the execution flow. Sometimes, you may want to terminate the loop prematurely or skip certain iterations of the loop based on certain conditions.

In Python, you can use the **break** and **continue** statements to modify the behavior of **for** and **while** loops. The **break** statement allows you to terminate the loop prematurely when a certain condition is met. For example, if you are searching for a particular value in a list, you can use the **break** statement to terminate the loop as soon as the value is found, instead of continuing to iterate through the rest of the list.

On the other hand, the **continue** statement allows you to skip certain iterations of the loop based on a certain condition. For example, if you are iterating through a list of numbers and you only want to process the even numbers, you can use the **continue** statement to skip over the odd numbers.

In this topic, we will discuss the use of these loop control statements and how they can be used effectively in different scenarios. By the end of this topic, you should have a better understanding of how to use **break** and **continue** statements in your Python programs to achieve more precise control over the execution flow of your loops.

4.3.1 break Statement:

The **break** statement is used to exit a loop prematurely, i.e., before the loop's condition becomes false or before iterating over all items in a sequence. When the **break** statement is encountered inside a loop, the loop is terminated immediately, and the program continues executing the code following the loop.

For example, let's say we want to search for a specific number in a list and stop the loop once the number is found:

```
numbers = [1, 2, 3, 4, 5]
search = 3

for number in numbers:
    if number == search:
        print("Found:", number)
        break
```

Code block: 4.15

Output:

```
Found: 3
```

Code block: 4.16

In this example, the loop stops iterating as soon as the search number is found, saving time and resources.

4.3.2 continue Statement:

The **continue** statement is used to skip the rest of the code inside a loop for the current iteration and jump to the next iteration. In other words, when the **continue** statement is encountered, Python skips the remaining code in the loop and moves to the next item in the sequence or evaluates the loop condition again.

For example, let's say we want to print all the numbers from 1 to 10, except for the multiples of 3:

```
for i in range(1, 11):
    if i % 3 == 0:
        continue
    print(i)
```

Code block: 4.17

Output:

```
1
2
4
5
7
8
10
```

Code block: 4.18

In this example, the loop skips printing the numbers that are divisible by 3 and continues with the next iteration.

In summary, loop control statements like **break** and **continue** can provide significant benefits in terms of control flow within loops. The **break** statement, for example, can be used to exit a loop prematurely if certain conditions are met. This can be particularly useful in situations where you want to stop iterating through a loop as soon as a specific condition is met, or if you want to exit the loop altogether. Similarly, the **continue** statement can be used to skip over specific iterations of a loop, which can help to optimize loop performance by avoiding unnecessary computation. By incorporating these control structures into your loops, you can make your code more efficient and readable, while also gaining greater control over the way your programs execute.

Exercise 4.3.1: Print First Five Even Numbers

In this exercise, you will write a Python program that prints the first five even numbers using a **for** loop and the **continue** statement.

Instructions:

1. Create a new Python file or open a Python interpreter.
2. Use a **for** loop to iterate through the numbers from 1 to 10 (inclusive).
3. Use an **if** statement to check if the current number is odd.
4. If the number is odd, use the **continue** statement to skip the rest of the code in the loop and move on to the next iteration.
5. Print the even number and increment a counter.
6. When the counter reaches 5, use the **break** statement to exit the loop.

Your final code should look something like this:

```python
counter = 0

for i in range(1, 11):
    if i % 2 != 0:
        continue
    print(i)
    counter += 1
    if counter == 5:
        break
```

Code block: E.4.3.1.1

Output:

```
2
4
6
8
10
```

Code block: E.4.3.1.2

Exercise 4.3.2: Sum of Positive Numbers

In this exercise, you will write a Python program that calculates the sum of all positive numbers in a list using a **for** loop and the **continue** statement.

Instructions:

1. Create a new Python file or open a Python interpreter.
2. Assign a list of integers (positive and negative) to a variable named **numbers**.
3. Initialize a variable named **total** with the value 0.
4. Use a **for** loop to iterate through the numbers in the list.
5. Use an **if** statement to check if the current number is negative.
6. If the number is negative, use the **continue** statement to skip the rest of the code in the loop and move on to the next iteration.
7. Add the positive number to the **total** variable.
8. Print the value of **total** after the loop is complete.

Your final code should look something like this:

```python
numbers = [1, -2, 3, -4, 5, -6, 7]
total = 0

for number in numbers:
    if number < 0:
        continue
    total += number

print(total)
```

Code block: E.4.3.2.1

Output:

```
16
```

Code block: E.4.3.2.2

Exercise 4.3.3: Find the First Factor

In this exercise, you will write a Python program that finds the first factor of a given number using a **for** loop and the **break** statement.

Instructions:

1. Create a new Python file or open a Python interpreter.
2. Assign an integer value to a variable named **n**.
3. Use a **for** loop to iterate through the numbers from 2 to **n** (inclusive).
4. Use an **if** statement to check if the current number is a factor of **n**.
5. If the number is a factor, print it and use the **break** statement to exit the loop.

Your final code should look something like this:

```python
n = 20

for i in range(2, n + 1):
    if n % i == 0:
        print("First factor:", i)
        break
```

Code block: E.4.3.3.1

Output:

```
First factor: 2
```

Code block: E.4.3.3.2

These exercises help you practice using the **break** and **continue** loop control statements in Python to control the flow of your programs and accomplish various tasks.

4.4: Nested Control Structures

As you advance in your Python programming skills, you will come across problems that require combining multiple control structures to find a solution. Nested control structures are one example of this, where you place one control structure inside another.

The use of nested control structures is essential for tackling more complex operations or manipulating multi-dimensional data. They help you to create more efficient and compact code that is simpler to understand and maintain. Furthermore, using nested control structures can help you to avoid repeating similar code blocks throughout your program, leading to less duplication and more streamlined code.

Overall, mastering the use of nested control structures is a must for any serious Python programmer looking to take their skills to the next level.

4.4.1: Nested Conditional Statements:

You can place an **if**, **elif**, or **else** block inside another **if**, **elif**, or **else** block. This creates nested conditional statements, which allow you to evaluate multiple conditions and choose the appropriate action based on the results.

For example, let's say we want to check the age and citizenship status of a person to determine if they are eligible to vote:

```python
age = 25
is_citizen = True

if age >= 18:
    if is_citizen:
        print("You are eligible to vote.")
    else:
        print("You must be a citizen to vote.")
else:
    print("You must be at least 18 years old to vote.")
```

Code block: 4.19

In this example, we first check if the person's age is greater than or equal to 18. If it is, we then check if they are a citizen. Depending on the results of these two conditions, the appropriate message is printed.

4.4.2: Nested Loops:

You can also nest loops within other loops. This is useful when you need to iterate over multi-dimensional data structures, like lists of lists or matrices. In nested loops, the inner loop iterates for each iteration of the outer loop.

For example, let's say we want to print the elements of a matrix:

```python
matrix = [
    [1, 2, 3],
    [4, 5, 6],
    [7, 8, 9]
]

for row in matrix:
    for element in row:
        print(element, end=" ")
    print()
```

Code block: 4.20

Output:

```
1 2 3
4 5 6
7 8 9
```

Code block: 4.21

In this example, the outer loop iterates through each row of the matrix, while the inner loop iterates through each element in the current row. This allows us to access and print each element of the matrix.

Nested control structures are a fundamental and crucial concept in Python programming. By using nested conditional statements and nested loops, it is possible to create complex logic that can handle and process multi-dimensional data. Furthermore, understanding and practicing nested control structures is essential in achieving proficiency in Python programming. As you become more familiar with Python, you will gain the ability to use nested control structures in innovative ways, such as in developing more efficient algorithms or creating advanced data structures that can be used in a variety of applications.

This knowledge will enable you to create more robust and scalable programs that can handle complex tasks and solve real-world problems. In addition, mastering nested control structures will also allow you to delve deeper into the inner workings of Python and gain a deeper understanding of how the language operates. This understanding can be applied to other programming languages as well, making it a valuable skill for any programmer to have.

Overall, learning and practicing nested control structures is a crucial step for anyone looking to become a proficient Python programmer, and it is an essential tool for creating high-quality, effective code.

Exercise 4.4.1: Grade Calculator

In this exercise, you will write a Python program that calculates the letter grade for a given percentage score using nested conditional statements.

Instructions:

1. Create a new Python file or open a Python interpreter.
2. Assign a percentage score to a variable named **score**.
3. Use nested conditional statements to determine the letter grade based on the following criteria:
    - A: 90-100
    - B: 80-89
    - C: 70-79
    - D: 60-69
    - F: 0-59
4. Print the letter grade.

Your final code should look something like this:

```
score = 85

if score >= 90:
    grade = "A"
elif score >= 80:
    grade = "B"
elif score >= 70:
    grade = "C"
elif score >= 60:
    grade = "D"
else:
    grade = "F"

print("Your grade is:", grade)
```

Code block: E.4.4.1.1

Output:

```
Your grade is: B
```

Code block: E.4.4.1.2

Exercise 4.4.2: Multiplication Table

In this exercise, you will write a Python program that prints a multiplication table using nested **for** loops.

Instructions:

1. Create a new Python file or open a Python interpreter.
2. Use a **for** loop to iterate through the numbers 1 to 10 (inclusive) as the outer loop.
3. Use another **for** loop inside the outer loop to iterate through the numbers 1 to 10 (inclusive) as the inner loop.
4. Multiply the current numbers of the outer and inner loops and print the result.
5. Format the output appropriately to display the multiplication table.

Your final code should look something like this:

```
for i in range(1, 11):
    for j in range(1, 11):
        print(i * j, end="\t")
    print()
```

Code block: E.4.4.2.1

Output:

```
1  2  3  4  5  6  7  8  9  10
2  4  6  8  10  12  14  16  18  20
3  6  9  12  15  18  21  24  27  30
...
10  20  30  40  50  60  70  80  90  100
```

Code block: E.4.4.2.2

Exercise 4.4.3: Triangle Pattern

In this exercise, you will write a Python program that prints a triangle pattern using nested **for** loops.

Instructions:

1. Create a new Python file or open a Python interpreter.
2. Assign an integer value to a variable named **n**, representing the number of rows in the triangle pattern.
3. Use a **for** loop to iterate through the numbers 1 to **n** (inclusive) as the outer loop.
4. Use another **for** loop inside the outer loop to iterate through the numbers 1 to the current number of the outer loop (inclusive) as the inner loop.
5. Print an asterisk (*) for each iteration of the inner loop.
6. After each iteration of the outer loop, print a newline to create a new row in the pattern.

Your final code should look something like this:

```
n = 5

for i in range(1, n + 1):
    for j in range(i):
        print("*", end=" ")
    print()
```

Code block: E.4.4.3.1

Output:

```
*
* *
* * *
* * * *
* * * * *
```

Code block: E.4.4.3.2

These exercises help you practice nested control structures in Python, allowing you to create more complex logic and handle multi-dimensional data.

CHAPTER 5: Functions

As you progress in your Python journey, you'll find that writing repetitive code can be time-consuming and prone to errors. By creating functions in Python, you can save time and reduce the risk of errors by reusing code that has already been created. Functions allow you to define a set of instructions that can be executed with specific input parameters, perform a specific action, and return a value. This can help you write more efficient and maintainable code, as you will be able to easily reuse and modify code as needed.

In this chapter, we will cover the fundamentals of defining and using functions. We will start by discussing the syntax for defining functions and the different types of arguments that can be passed to a function. We will also show you how to use return statements to return values from a function. Finally, we will demonstrate how to call functions and use them in your code to make it more efficient and modular.

By the end of this chapter, you should have a solid understanding of how to define and use functions in Python. This knowledge will be essential as you continue to develop your Python skills and tackle more complex programming challenges in the future.

5.1: Defining Functions

A function in Python is a building block of any program, and it is designed to perform a specific, isolated task. The main advantage of using functions lies in the fact that they promote better modularity, which means that your code is more organized and easier to work with. In addition, functions help to make your code more understandable, maintainable, and debuggable, which can save you a lot of time and frustration in the long run.

Moreover, the use of functions can help you to avoid writing redundant code, which can be a big problem for large projects. By breaking your code into small, manageable pieces, you can create a more efficient and streamlined program that is easier to read and maintain. Overall, functions are an essential part of any Python program, and mastering them is key to becoming a proficient developer.

To define a function in Python, you use the **def** keyword, followed by the function name, a pair of parentheses (), and a colon :. The function body is indented, just like other code blocks in Python. The general syntax for defining a function is as follows:

```python
def function_name():
    # Function body
```

Code block: 5.1

Here's an example of a simple function that prints "Hello, World!":

```python
def hello_world():
    print("Hello, World!")

# Calling the function
hello_world()
```

Code block: 5.2

When you run this code, it will output "Hello, World!". Notice that we defined the function **hello_world** using the **def** keyword and then called the function by typing its name followed by parentheses.

Functions can also accept input parameters, which are specified inside the parentheses when defining the function. You can pass one or multiple parameters, separated by commas. Here's an example of a function that accepts a parameter:

```python
def greet(name):
    print(f"Hello, {name}!")

# Calling the function with an argument
greet("Alice")
```

Code block: 5.3

When you run this code, it will output "Hello, Alice!". In this example, the function **greet** accepts a single parameter called **name**. When we call the function, we pass the value "Alice" as an argument to the **name** parameter.

In the next topics, we will learn more about using parameters, returning values, and working with different types of functions in Python. But for now, you have learned the basics of defining and using functions to organize your code and make it more modular and reusable.

Exercise 5.1.1: Simple Greeting Function

Create a function that takes a name as an input parameter and prints a personalized greeting message.

Instructions:

1. Define a function called **greet** that accepts one parameter, **name**.
2. Inside the function, print a greeting message using the **name** parameter.
3. Call the function with your name as the argument.

Solution:

```python
def greet(name):
    print(f"Hello, {name}!")

greet("John")
```

Code block: E.5.1.1.1

Output:

```
Hello, John!
```

Code block: E.5.1.1.2

Exercise 5.1.2: Sum of Two Numbers

Create a function that takes two numbers as input parameters and prints their sum.

Instructions:

1. Define a function called **add** that accepts two parameters, **num1** and **num2**.
2. Inside the function, calculate the sum of **num1** and **num2**.
3. Print the result.
4. Call the function with two numbers of your choice as arguments.

Solution:

```python
def add(num1, num2):
    result = num1 + num2
    print(f"The sum of {num1} and {num2} is {result}.")

add(5, 7)
```

Code block: E.5.1.2.1

Output:

```
The sum of 5 and 7 is 12.
```

Code block: E.5.1.2.2

Exercise 5.1.3: Area of a Rectangle

Create a function that takes the length and width of a rectangle as input parameters and prints the area of the rectangle.

Instructions:

1. Define a function called **rectangle_area** that accepts two parameters, **length** and **width**.
2. Inside the function, calculate the area of the rectangle using the formula: area = length * width.
3. Print the area.
4. Call the function with the length and width of a rectangle of your choice as arguments.

Solution:

```python
def rectangle_area(length, width):
    area = length * width
    print(f"The area of the rectangle with length {length} and width {width} is {area}.")

rectangle_area(10, 5)
```

Code block: E.5.1.3.1

Output:

```
The area of the rectangle with length 10 and width 5 is 50.
```

Code block: E.5.1.3.2

5.2: Function Arguments

In the previous topic, we introduced the concept of functions and how to define them with input parameters. However, to fully understand functions, it is important to have a deeper understanding of the different types of function arguments in Python.

First, let's talk about positional arguments. These are the most common type of argument in Python functions. They are called "positional" because their values are assigned based on the order in which the arguments are passed to the function. For example, if a function has two positional arguments, the first value passed in will be assigned to the first argument and the second value passed in will be assigned to the second argument.

Now, let's move on to keyword arguments. These arguments are identified by the parameter name in the function definition. They are useful for making the code more readable and for providing default values to arguments.

Another type of argument is default arguments. These arguments have default values assigned to them, so if a value is not passed in for them when the function is called, the default value will be used. This is useful when a function is called frequently with the same value and you want to avoid having to pass in that value each time.

Finally, there are variable-length arguments. These arguments are denoted by an asterisk (*) before the parameter name. They allow a function to accept an arbitrary number of arguments. This is useful when you don't know how many arguments will be passed to the function ahead of time.

So, to summarize, Python has four main types of function arguments: positional arguments, keyword arguments, default arguments, and variable-length arguments. By understanding these different types of arguments, you will be able to write more flexible and powerful functions that can handle a variety of inputs.

5.2.1: Positional arguments:

Positional arguments are the most common type of function arguments. They are passed to a function in the same order in which they are defined in the function. The number of arguments passed to the function must match the number of parameters defined.

In contrast to other types of function arguments, such as keyword arguments and default arguments, positional arguments are the most straightforward and widely used. They are simple to understand and use, as they only require passing values in a specific order. However, they can pose a challenge if the number of arguments passed to the function does not match the number of parameters defined. In such cases, the function will raise a TypeError, indicating that the number of arguments expected does not match the number of arguments received.

One way to avoid this issue is to carefully define the number of parameters in the function's definition and ensure that the number of arguments passed to the function matches this number. Another way is to use other types of function arguments, such as keyword arguments or default arguments, which provide more flexibility in terms of the number and order of arguments passed to the function. However, these types of arguments may be more complex and require additional understanding and practice to use effectively.

Example:

```python
def person_info(name, age, city):
    print(f"{name} is {age} years old and lives in {city}.")

person_info("Alice", 25, "New York")
```

Code block: 5.4

Output:

```
Alice is 25 years old and lives in New York.
```

Code block: 5.5

5.2.2: Keyword arguments:

Keyword arguments are an essential feature of Python functions. They let you pass arguments to a function using parameter names, making the code more readable and easier to understand. This is especially useful when functions have many arguments, and it is challenging to remember the order in which they have to be passed.

For example, suppose you have a function that takes five arguments, and you want to pass only the 3rd and 5th arguments. With keyword arguments, you can do this easily by specifying the parameter names for those arguments. This way, you don't have to worry about the order in which the arguments are defined in the function.

Another benefit of keyword arguments is that they make the function more flexible. You can pass arguments in any order, regardless of their position in the function. This is particularly useful when you want to reuse a function with different argument values, and you don't want to modify the function's code to accommodate the new arguments.

Keyword arguments are a powerful tool that can help you write cleaner, more efficient code. They make functions more readable, flexible, and easier to use, making your job as a programmer much more comfortable and enjoyable.

Example:

```
def person_info(name, age, city):
    print(f"{name} is {age} years old and lives in {city}.")

person_info(age=25, city="New York", name="Alice")
```

Code block: 5.6

Output:

```
Alice is 25 years old and lives in New York.
```

Code block: 5.7

5.2.3: Default arguments:

Default arguments have an important feature that can simplify the implementation of functions in many programming languages. This feature allows you to assign a default value to a parameter, making it optional when calling the function. By doing this, you avoid the need to define and implement multiple functions that perform the same operation with different numbers of arguments.

This feature is particularly useful when a function is called in many different ways, since it allows you to avoid having to write many different versions of the same function. This can save a lot of time and make your code easier to maintain. Additionally, default arguments can make your code more readable by reducing the number of conditional statements needed to handle different argument configurations.

Therefore, it is recommended to use default arguments whenever possible, especially when you need to write functions that can handle a large number of argument configurations. If the caller does not provide a value for the parameter, the default value will be used, ensuring that the function works correctly even if the caller forgets to provide all the necessary arguments.

Example:

```python
def person_info(name, age, city="Unknown"):
    print(f"{name} is {age} years old and lives in {city}.")

person_info("Alice", 25)
```

Code block: 5.8

Output:

```
Alice is 25 years old and lives in Unknown.
```

Code block: 5.9

5.2.4: Variable-length arguments:

Variable-length arguments are a powerful feature in programming languages, as they allow you to pass an arbitrary number of arguments to a function. This means that you can write code that is more flexible and adaptable to various use cases. This feature becomes especially useful when you do not know the exact number of arguments you'll be passing to a function.

In Python, you can use the asterisk (*) for tuples, which are used to pass positional arguments, and double asterisks (**) for dictionaries, which are used to pass keyword arguments. When using variable-length arguments, it is important to keep in mind that you can pass as many arguments as you want, but you need to make sure that your function can handle them all.

Overall, variable-length arguments are an essential tool for any programmer, as they provide a way to write more flexible and adaptable code, without being limited by the number of arguments that a function can accept.

Example:

```python
def print_names(*names):
    for name in names:
        print(name)

print_names("Alice", "Bob", "Charlie", "David")
```

Code block: 5.10

Output:

```
Alice
Bob
Charlie
David
```

Code block: 5.11

To master the art of writing flexible and efficient functions in Python, it is crucial to have a solid grasp of the various types of function arguments. Whether you're passing in default arguments, keyword arguments, or variable-length arguments, each type offers unique benefits and trade-offs that can impact the overall performance and functionality of your code.

In the next topic, we will dive deeper into the topic of returning values from functions. Not only will we explore the basic syntax and mechanics of returning values, but we will also examine real-world examples of how to leverage return values to enhance the power and versatility of your functions. By the end of this topic, you'll have a comprehensive understanding of how to use return values to take your Python code to the next level.

Exercise 5.2.1: Simple Calculator

Create a simple calculator that takes two numbers and an arithmetic operation as input and performs the operation on the two numbers.

Instructions:

1. Define a function called **simple_calculator** that takes three parameters: **num1**, **num2**, and **operation**.
2. Use an if-elif-else structure to perform the corresponding operation based on the input (addition, subtraction, multiplication, or division).
3. Print the result of the operation.
4. Call the function with different arguments to test the calculator.

Solution:

```python
def simple_calculator(num1, num2, operation):
    if operation == "add":
        result = num1 + num2
    elif operation == "subtract":
        result = num1 - num2
    elif operation == "multiply":
        result = num1 * num2
    elif operation == "divide":
        result = num1 / num2
    else:
        result = "Invalid operation"
    print(result)

simple_calculator(5, 3, "add")
simple_calculator(5, 3, "subtract")
simple_calculator(5, 3, "multiply")
simple_calculator(5, 3, "divide")
```

Code block: E.5.2.1.1

Output:

```
8
2
15
1.6666666666666667
```

Code block: E.5.2.1.2

Exercise 5.2.2: Greeting with Default Argument

Create a function that greets a user by their name. If the name is not provided, the function should greet a generic user.

Instructions:

1. Define a function called **greet** that takes one parameter, **name**, with a default value of "User".
2. Print a greeting message that includes the name.
3. Call the function with a name and without a name to test the default argument.

Solution:

```python
def greet(name="User"):
    print(f"Hello, {name}!")

greet("Alice")
greet()
```

Code block: E.5.2.2.1

Output:

```
Hello, Alice!
Hello, User!
```

Code block: E.5.2.2.2

Exercise 5.2.3: Sum of Numbers with Variable-length Arguments

Create a function that calculates the sum of an arbitrary number of numbers passed as arguments.

Instructions:

1. Define a function called **sum_of_numbers** that takes variable-length arguments using the asterisk (*).
2. Initialize a variable called **total** to store the sum.
3. Iterate through the arguments and add each number to the total.
4. Print the total sum.
5. Call the function with different numbers of arguments to test the variable-length arguments.

Solution:

```python
def sum_of_numbers(*numbers):
    total = 0
    for number in numbers:
        total += number
    print(total)

sum_of_numbers(1, 2, 3, 4, 5)
sum_of_numbers(10, 20, 30)
sum_of_numbers(100, 200)
```

Code block: E.5.2.3.1

Output:

```
15
60
300
```

Code block: E.5.2.3.2

5.3: Return Values

In the previous topics, we have covered the essentials of defining functions and function arguments. In this topic, we will delve deeper into the concept of return values.

Return values are an integral part of Python functions. When a function is executed, it can return a value to the caller. This value can then be used for further processing or passed on as input to another function.

To return a value from a function, the **return** statement is used, which is followed by the value or expression that needs to be returned. It is important to note that the **return** statement marks the end of the function, and the control is then passed back to the caller. This feature is particularly useful when you want to avoid repeated code or when you want to pass on a result to another function.

The general syntax for a function with a return value is:

```python
def function_name(parameters):
    ...
    return value
```

Code block: 5.12

Let's take a look at some examples to better understand how return values work.

Example 1: Simple addition function

```python
def add(a, b):
    result = a + b
    return result

sum_result = add(5, 7)
print(sum_result)   # Output: 12
```

Code block: 5.13

In this example, the **add** function takes two parameters, **a** and **b**, adds them together, and returns the result. When we call the **add** function with the arguments 5 and 7, the returned value (12) is assigned to the variable **sum_result**.

Example 2: Maximum of two numbers

```python
def maximum(a, b):
    if a > b:
        return a
    else:
        return b

max_value = maximum(10, 15)
print(max_value)   # Output: 15
```

Code block: 5.14

Here, we define a **maximum** function that takes two parameters, **a** and **b**, and returns the greater one. The function uses an if-else statement to determine which value is greater and returns it accordingly.

Example 3: Return multiple values

You can also return multiple values from a function using a tuple, list, or dictionary.

```python
def min_max(numbers):
    return min(numbers), max(numbers)

values = [5, 2, 8, 1, 10]
minimum, maximum = min_max(values)
print(f"Minimum: {minimum}, Maximum: {maximum}")  # Output: Minimum: 1, Maximum: 10
```

Code block. 5.15

In this example, we have a function **min_max** that takes a list of numbers as input and returns a tuple containing the minimum and maximum values. When the function is called with a list, it returns the tuple, which we then unpack into the **minimum** and **maximum** variables.

Remember that once a **return** statement is executed, the function exits immediately. If there is code after the return statement, it won't be executed.

Exercise 5.3.1: Calculate Area of a Rectangle

Write a function called **area_of_rectangle** that takes two arguments, **length** and **width**, and returns the area of a rectangle.

Instructions:

1. Define the function **area_of_rectangle**.
2. Calculate the area of the rectangle.
3. Return the calculated area.

Solution:

```python
def area_of_rectangle(length, width):
    area = length * width
    return area

length = 5
width = 10
result = area_of_rectangle(length, width)
print(f"The area of the rectangle is {result}")   # Output: The area of the rectangle is 50
```

Code block: E.5.3.1.1

Exercise 5.3.2: Check if a Number is Even or Odd

Create a function called **is_even** that takes a single argument, **number**, and returns **True** if the number is even and **False** otherwise.

Instructions:

1. Define the function **is_even**.
2. Use the modulo operator to check if the number is even.
3. Return **True** if the number is even and **False** otherwise.

Solution:

```python
def is_even(number):
    if number % 2 == 0:
        return True
    else:
        return False

num = 7
result = is_even(num)
print(f"Is {num} even? {result}")   # Output: Is 7 even? False
```

Code block: E.5.3.2.1

Exercise 5.3.3: Get the Length of a String

Write a function called **string_length** that takes a single argument, **string**, and returns the length of the string.

Instructions:

1. Define the function **string_length**.
2. Use the **len()** function to find the length of the string.
3. Return the length of the string.

```
def string_length(string):
    length = len(string)
    return length

text = "Python is awesome!"
result = string_length(text)
print(f"The length of the string is {result}")   # Output: The length of the string is 18
```

Code block: E.5.3.3.1

5.4: Scope of Variables

In Python, it's important to understand the visibility and accessibility of a variable, which depends on its scope. Scope refers to the area in your code where a variable can be accessed or used. By understanding variable scope, you can write efficient and error-free code. Python has two main types of variable scopes:

5.4.1: Global scope:

A variable declared outside a function or a block of code has global scope. This means that you can access the variable from anywhere in the code, including within functions. However, modifying the value of a global variable inside a function is not recommended unless you use the **global** keyword.

Understanding the difference between global and local scope is essential for writing effective Python code. By using the appropriate scope for your variables, you can ensure that your code is efficient and easy to read.

Example:

```python
global_var = "I am a global variable"

def my_function():
    print(global_var)

my_function()   # Output: I am a global variable
```

Code block: 5.16

5.4.2: Local scope:

A variable declared inside a function or block of code has a local scope, which means that it can only be accessed within that function or block of code. This is a useful feature because it allows us to keep variables contained within a specific section of our code, avoiding any potential conflicts with other variables that may have the same name.

However, it is important to note that once the function or block of code finishes its execution, the local variable is destroyed and cannot be accessed anymore. This is why it is crucial to properly manage the scope of your variables, ensuring that they are accessible when and where they are needed, but not kept around unnecessarily after their use has ended.

Example:

```python
def my_function():
    local_var = "I am a local variable"
    print(local_var)

my_function()   # Output: I am a local variable
print(local_var)  # Error: local_var is not defined in the global scope
```

Code block: 5.17

It's important to note that if a local variable has the same name as a global variable, the local variable takes precedence inside the function. This means that any operations performed on the variable inside the function will not affect the global variable.

Example:

```
x = 10

def modify_x():
    x = 5
    print(f"Inside the function, x is {x}")

modify_x()  # Output: Inside the function, x is 5
print(f"Outside the function, x is {x}")  # Output: Outside the function, x is 10
```

Code block: 5.18

In summary, understanding the scope of variables is crucial for managing data throughout your code. Global variables can be accessed anywhere in the code but should be used sparingly, while local variables are restricted to their respective functions or blocks of code.

Exercise 5.4.1: Accessing Global Variables Inside a Function

In this exercise, you will practice accessing a global variable inside a function without modifying it.

Instructions:

1. Create a global variable called **name** and assign it the value "John".
2. Define a function called **print_name** that prints the global variable **name**.
3. Call the **print_name** function.

Solution:

```python
name = "John"

def print_name():
    print(name)

print_name()
```

Code block: E.5.4.1.1

Output:

```
John
```

Code block: E.5.4.1.2

Exercise 5.4.2: Modifying Global Variables Inside a Function

In this exercise, you will practice modifying a global variable inside a function using the **global** keyword.

Instructions:

1. Create a global variable called **counter** and assign it the value 0.
2. Define a function called **increment_counter** that increments the global variable **counter** by 1.
3. Call the **increment_counter** function three times.
4. Print the value of **counter**.

Solution:

```
counter = 0

def increment_counter():
    global counter
    counter += 1

increment_counter()
increment_counter()
increment_counter()

print(counter)
```

Code block: E.5.4.2.1

Output:

```
3
```

Code block: E.5.4.2.2

Exercise 5.4.3: Local Variables vs. Global Variables

In this exercise, you will practice using both local and global variables with the same name and observe their behavior inside and outside a function.

Instructions:

1. Create a global variable called **message** and assign it the value "Global message".

2. Define a function called **print_local_message** that: a. Creates a local variable called **message** with the value "Local message". b. Prints the local variable **message**.
3. Call the **print_local_message** function.
4. Print the global variable **message**.

Solution:

```python
message = "Global message"

def print_local_message():
    message = "Local message"
    print(message)

print_local_message()
print(message)
```

Code block: E.5.4.3.1

Output:

```
Local message
Global message
```

Code block: E.5.4.3.2

5.5: Lambda Functions

In this section, we will introduce lambda functions, a concise way of creating small, anonymous functions. Lambda functions are particularly useful for simple operations that can be defined in a single line of code.

Lambda functions can be used for a variety of purposes, from filtering data to sorting values. They can also be used to manipulate data in various ways, such as mapping values to a new data structure or reducing data to a single value. The versatility of lambda functions makes them a valuable tool for any programmer.

When creating a lambda function, it's important to keep in mind that they are anonymous functions, meaning they do not have a name. This can make them difficult to debug if an error occurs. However, the benefits of using lambda functions often outweigh the potential drawbacks.

To create a lambda function, you start with the **lambda** keyword, followed by the function's input parameters and a colon. After the colon, you provide the expression that represents the function's logic. It's important to note that lambda functions can have any number of input parameters but can only have one expression. This expression should be concise but still fully represent the function's intended logic.

Overall, lambda functions are a powerful tool for any programmer looking to write concise, efficient code. With their ability to handle a variety of tasks and their simple syntax, lambda functions are a valuable addition to any programmer's toolset.

Syntax:

```
lambda parameters: expression
```

Code block: 5.19

Example:

```
# Regular function
def add(a, b):
    return a + b

result = add(2, 3)
print(result)   # Output: 5

# Equivalent lambda function
add_lambda = lambda a, b: a + b

result_lambda = add_lambda(2, 3)
print(result_lambda)   # Output: 5
```

Code block: 5.20

In the example above, we define a regular function called **add** that takes two parameters **a** and **b** and returns their sum. Then, we define a lambda function called **add_lambda** that does the same thing. Both functions produce the same result when called with the same arguments.

When it comes to working with lambda functions, there are some limitations that are important to keep in mind. While they can be incredibly useful for small, simple operations, they are not well-suited for more complex tasks. This is because lambda functions are restricted to having just one expression, and they cannot include statements, assignments, or multiple expressions that need to be combined.

Despite these limitations, lambda functions are still quite valuable in many contexts. For example, they can be used as arguments for higher-order functions, such as **map()**, **filter()**, or **sorted()**. These functions take other functions as input, and lambda functions can be used to provide these input functions. By using lambda functions in this way, it becomes possible to accomplish a wide variety of tasks.

In the next section, we will provide a series of practical exercises that are designed to help you solidify your understanding of lambda functions. These exercises will allow you to put your newfound knowledge to the test, and will provide you with valuable experience using lambda functions in a range of different contexts.

Exercise 5.5.1: Lambda Square

Create a lambda function that takes a single number as input and returns its square.

Instructions:

1. Define a lambda function that takes one parameter.
2. Write an expression that calculates the square of the input.
3. Test the lambda function with a number of your choice.

Solution:

```python
square = lambda x: x**2

result = square(4)
print(result)  # Output: 16
```

Code block: E.5.5.1.1

Exercise 5.5.2: Lambda List Sorting

Sort a list of tuples based on the second element of each tuple using a lambda function.

Instructions:

1. Create a list of tuples containing two numbers each.
2. Use the **sorted()** function with a lambda function as the **key** argument.
3. Print the sorted list.

Solution:

```
data = [(1, 3), (5, 2), (7, 1), (3, 4)]
sorted_data = sorted(data, key=lambda x: x[1])

print(sorted_data)   # Output: [(7, 1), (5, 2), (1, 3), (3, 4)]
```

Code block: E.5.5.2.1

Exercise 5.5.3: Lambda with Filter

Use a lambda function with the **filter()** function to find all even numbers in a list.

Instructions:

1. Create a list of integers.
2. Use the **filter()** function with a lambda function that checks if a number is even.
3. Convert the filtered result to a list and print it.

Solution:

```python
numbers = [1, 2, 3, 4, 5, 6, 7, 8, 9]
even_numbers = list(filter(lambda x: x % 2 == 0, numbers))

print(even_numbers)  # Output: [2, 4, 6, 8]
```

Code block: E.5.5.3.1

We've now reached the end of Chapter 5, "Functions". Throughout this chapter, we've explored various concepts related to functions, including defining functions, function arguments, return values, the scope of variables, and lambda functions. These concepts are essential in helping you write clean, reusable, and efficient code.

We hope the detailed explanations and practical exercises have helped you to not only understand these concepts but also apply them in your Python programming journey. As you continue to practice and work through the exercises, you'll become more comfortable using functions to create well-structured code.

In the upcoming chapters, we will delve deeper into Python's rich features and libraries, covering topics such as data structures, modules, and object-oriented programming. Keep up the enthusiasm, and don't hesitate to revisit previous chapters if you need a refresher on any of the concepts.

CHAPTER 6: Working with Files

In this chapter, we will explore how to work with files in Python. Files are an essential part of most programming projects, as they allow you to store, retrieve, and manipulate data outside your program. By learning to work with files, you will be able to create more complex and data-driven applications.

One important aspect of working with files is learning how to handle errors. When opening a file, it is possible that the file does not exist or that the user does not have permission to access it. In these cases, your program should be able to handle the error gracefully and provide feedback to the user.

Another important concept is understanding the different file modes available. These modes determine how the file can be accessed and modified. For example, the "r" mode allows you to read the contents of a file, while the "w" mode allows you to write new data to a file.

We will also cover how to read and write different file types. Additionally, we will explore how to use the os module to interact with the file system and perform tasks such as creating directories and deleting files.

By the end of this chapter, you will have a solid understanding of how to work with files in Python and be able to apply this knowledge to your own programming projects.

6.1: Opening and Closing Files

To start working with files in Python, you need to understand how to open and close them. The built-in **open()** function is used to open a file, and it returns a file object which you can use to perform various operations on the file.

The **open()** function takes two main arguments:

1. The file name (including the path if the file is not located in the same directory as your script).
2. The mode in which the file should be opened.

There are several modes you can use when opening a file:

- **'r'**: Read mode, for reading the contents of an existing file (default mode if not specified).
- **'w'**: Write mode, for creating a new file or overwriting the contents of an existing file.
- **'a'**: Append mode, for appending data to an existing file without overwriting its content.
- **'x'**: Exclusive creation mode, for creating a new file but raising an error if the file already exists.

You can also specify if the file should be treated as a binary file by adding a **'b'** to the mode, like **'rb'**, **'wb'**, etc.

Here's an example of how to open a file in read mode:

```python
file = open("example.txt", "r")p
```

Code block: 6.1

Once you have finished working with a file, it's essential to close it properly. Closing a file ensures that any changes made to it are saved and that system resources are freed up. You can close a file using the **close()** method of the file object:

```python
file.close()
```

Code block: 6.2

It's a good practice to use the **with** statement when working with files, as it automatically takes care of closing the file for you when the block of code is finished. The **with** statement is also known as a context manager. Here's an example:

```
with open("example.txt", "r") as file:
    # Perform file operations here
    pass
```

Code block. 6.3

In this example, the **with** statement creates a context where the file is opened, and after the block of code is executed, the file is automatically closed.

Now that you have a solid understanding of the fundamental concepts behind opening and closing files, including the various file modes that are available, it's time to delve deeper into the topic and explore how to read and write data to files.

In the upcoming sections, we will discuss techniques for reading data from files, including how to read data in various formats. We will also cover the process of writing data to files, including how to write data in different formats and how to append data to existing files.

In addition, we'll explore some advanced file input and output techniques, such as handling binary data and working with large files. By the end of these sections, you'll have a comprehensive understanding of how to work with files in your Python programs.

Exercise 6.1.1: Create a new file

Write a Python program that creates a new text file and writes a line of text to it.

Instructions:

1. Use the **open()** function to create a new text file named **new_file.txt** in write mode.
2. Write the line **"Hello, World!"** to the file.
3. Close the file.

Solution:

```
with open("new_file.txt", "w") as file:
    file.write("Hello, World!")
```

Code block: E.6.1.1.1

Output: A new file named **new_file.txt** will be created with the content **"Hello, World!"**.

Exercise 6.1.2: Read a file

Write a Python program that reads the content of a text file and prints it to the console.

Instructions:

1. Create a text file named **input.txt** containing some lines of text.
2. Use the **open()** function to open the file in read mode.
3. Read the content of the file using the **read()** method.
4. Print the content of the file to the console.
5. Close the file.

Solution:

First, create the **input.txt** file with some content:

```
This is a sample text file.
It contains several lines of text.
```

Code block: E.6.1.2.1

Then, the Python code:

```
with open("input.txt", "r") as file:
    content = file.read()
    print(content)
```

Code block: E.6.1.2.2

Output:

```
This is a sample text file.
It contains several lines of text.
```

Code block: E.6.1.2.3

Exercise 6.1.3: Append to a file

Title: Append to a file

Description: Write a Python program that appends a new line of text to an existing text file.

Instructions:

1. Create a text file named **append_file.txt** containing a single line of text: **"Original line\\n"**.
2. Use the **open()** function to open the file in append mode.
3. Write a new line of text: **"Appended line"** to the file.
4. Close the file.

Solution:

First, create the **append_file.txt** file with the initial content:

```
Original line
```

Code block: E.6.1.3.1

Then, the Python code:

```python
with open("append_file.txt", "a") as file:
    file.write("Appended line")
```

Code block: E.6.1.3.2

Output: The file **append_file.txt** will now have the following content:

```
Original line
Appended line
```

Code block: E.6.1.3.3

6.2: Reading and Writing Files

In this section, we will discuss different ways to read and write data to and from files. We have already seen how to open a file and read its content or write data to it. Now, let's explore some additional methods that make reading and writing files more efficient and convenient.

6.2.1: Reading files line by line:

Reading a file line by line is a common task, especially when dealing with large text files. This can be done using the **readline()** method or by iterating through the file object.

Example:

```python
with open("file.txt", "r") as file:
    for line in file:
        print(line.strip())
```

Code block: 6.4

In this example, we open the file in read mode and iterate over each line using a for loop. The **strip()** method is used to remove any leading and trailing whitespace (like newline characters) from the line before printing.

6.2.2: Writing multiple lines to a file:

When writing multiple lines to a file, you can use the **writelines()** method. This method takes a list of strings as input and writes them to the file as separate lines.

Example:

```python
lines = ["Line 1\n", "Line 2\n", "Line 3\n"]
with open("file.txt", "w") as file:
    file.writelines(lines)
```

Code block: 6.5

In this example, we open the file in write mode and write the list of strings **lines** to the file using the **writelines()** method. Note that newline characters (**\n**) are added to the end of each string to ensure that each line is written on a new line.

6.2.3: Reading and writing binary files:

Sometimes, you may need to work with binary files, like images or executables. To read and write binary files, you need to open the file in binary mode by adding a "b" to the mode parameter. The methods for reading and writing remain the same, but the data is treated as bytes instead of strings.

Example:

```python
# Copy a binary file
with open("source.jpg", "rb") as source_file:
    data = source_file.read()

with open("destination.jpg", "wb") as destination_file:
    destination_file.write(data)
```

Code block: 6.6

In this example, we open a binary file (an image) in read-binary mode, read its content, and then write the content to a new binary file in write-binary mode.

In conclusion, Python offers a wide range of methods for reading and writing files. These methods can be used to handle data in multiple formats and for various purposes, from simple text files to complex databases.

By mastering these techniques, you will be able to manipulate data in powerful ways and streamline your programming tasks. Additionally, Python's file handling capabilities are not limited to just reading and writing data.

You can also use Python to create, delete, and modify files, as well as manage directories and file permissions. As you become more proficient and comfortable with Python, you will undoubtedly discover new and innovative ways to use its file handling features in your programming projects.

Exercise 6.2.1: Counting Lines in a Text File

Instructions:

1. Create a text file named "sample.txt" with multiple lines of text.
2. Write a Python program to open the file, read its content, and count the number of lines.
3. Print the total number of lines.

Solution:

```python
line_count = 0

with open("sample.txt", "r") as file:
    for line in file:
        line_count += 1

print(f"Total number of lines: {line_count}")
```

Code block: E.6.2.1.1

Output:

```
Total number of lines: <number_of_lines_in_sample.txt>
```

Code block: E.6.2.1.2

Exercise 6.2.2: Reversing Lines in a Text File

In this exercise, you will read a text file, reverse the order of the lines, and write the reversed content to a new text file.

Instructions:

1. Create a text file named "original.txt" with multiple lines of text.

2. Write a Python program to open the file, read its content, and reverse the order of the lines.
3. Write the reversed content to a new text file named "reversed.txt".

Solution:

```
with open("original.txt", "r") as original_file:
    lines = original_file.readlines()

lines.reverse()

with open("reversed.txt", "w") as reversed_file:
    reversed_file.writelines(lines)
```

Code block: E.6.2.2.1

Exercise 6.2.3: Read and Write a Binary File

In this exercise, you will read a binary file (e.g., an image) and write its content to a new binary file.

Instructions:

1. Choose a binary file (e.g., an image) named "source.bin".
2. Write a Python program to open the binary file, read its content, and write the content to a new binary file named "destination.bin".

Solution:

```
with open("source.bin", "rb") as source_file:
    data = source_file.read()

with open("destination.bin", "wb") as destination_file:
    destination_file.write(data)
```

Code block: E.6.2.3.1

After executing the solution code, you should find a new binary file named "destination.bin" in your working directory, which is an exact copy of the "source.bin" file.

6.3: File Modes and Operations

When working with files in Python, it is essential to understand the different file modes and operations available. File modes determine how you can interact with a file (e.g., reading, writing, or appending), while file operations refer to the actions you perform on a file (e.g., reading content, writing content, or seeking a specific position).

Here's a detailed explanation of common file modes:

1. 'r': Read mode - In this mode, the file is opened for reading. You can only read the file's content, and the file must exist before opening. If the file doesn't exist, a FileNotFoundError will be raised.
2. 'w': Write mode - In this mode, the file is opened for writing. If the file doesn't exist, it will be created. If it already exists, its content will be overwritten (i.e., truncated).
3. 'a': Append mode - In this mode, the file is opened for appending. If the file doesn't exist, it will be created. If it already exists, new data will be added to the end of the file, preserving the original content.
4. 'x': Exclusive creation mode - In this mode, the file is opened for exclusive creation. If the file already exists, an error will be raised. If it doesn't exist, a new file will be created.
5. 'b': Binary mode - This mode is used for binary files, such as images or executables. By adding the 'b' mode to any other mode (e.g., 'rb', 'wb', 'ab'), the file will be treated as a binary file.
6. 't': Text mode - This mode is used for text files. By adding the 't' mode to any other mode (e.g., 'rt', 'wt', 'at'), the file will be treated as a text file. By default, if no mode is specified, Python assumes 't' mode.

You can combine modes to achieve the desired effect. For example, 'r+' opens a file for both reading and writing, while 'rb' opens a file for reading in binary mode.

Some common file operations include:

1. **read()**: Read the entire content of the file as a single string (or as bytes in binary mode).
2. **readline()**: Read a single line from the file.
3. **readlines()**: Read all lines from the file into a list.
4. **write()**: Write a string (or bytes in binary mode) to the file.
5. **writelines()**: Write a list of strings (or bytes in binary mode) to the file.
6. **seek()**: Move the file pointer to a specific position in the file.

7. **tell()**: Get the current position of the file pointer.

Remember to close a file once you're done with it, either by calling the **close()** method or by using the **with** statement, which automatically closes the file when the block of code is exited. Properly closing a file ensures that any changes are saved and resources are released.

Here's a code example that demonstrates some of the file modes and operations we discussed in the previous explanation:

```python
# Writing a file in write mode
with open("example.txt", "w") as f:
    f.write("This is an example file.\n")
    f.write("We are writing some content here.\n")

# Reading a file in read mode
with open("example.txt", "r") as f:
    content = f.read()
    print("Content of the file:")
    print(content)

# Appending content to the file in append mode
with open("example.txt", "a") as f:
    f.write("This line is appended to the file.\n")

# Reading the file again after appending
with open("example.txt", "r") as f:
    content = f.read()
    print("Content of the file after appending:")
    print(content)

# Demonstrating file operations
with open("example.txt", "r") as f:
    # Read a single line
    first_line = f.readline()
    print("First line:", first_line.strip())

    # Read all lines into a list
    f.seek(0)  # Move the file pointer back to the start of the file
    lines = f.readlines()
    print("All lines:", lines)

    # Get the current position of the file pointer
    position = f.tell()
    print("Current position of the file pointer:", position)
```

Code block: 6.7

Output:

```
Content of the file:
This is an example file.
We are writing some content here.

Content of the file after appending:
This is an example file.
We are writing some content here.
This line is appended to the file.

First line: This is an example file.
All lines: ['This is an example file.\n', 'We are writing some content here.\n', 'This line is appended to the file.\n']
Current position of the file pointer: 82
```

Code block: 6.8

To complete the next exercises, please visit cuantum.tech/books/python-beginner/chapter6/ and download the files required for each exercise.

Exercise 6.3.1: Counting Lines in a File

Create a program that reads a given file and prints the number of lines in the file.

Instructions:

1. Read the provided "sample_text.txt" file.
2. Count the number of lines in the file.
3. Print the number of lines.

Solution:

```python
filename = "sample_text.txt"

with open(filename, "r") as f:
    lines = f.readlines()
    line_count = len(lines)

print(f"The number of lines in the file is: {line_count}")
```

Code block: E.6.3.1.1

Output:

```
The number of lines in the file is: 4
```

Code block: E.6.3.1.2

The "sample_text.txt" file has the following content:

```
This is a sample file.
It contains some text.
Here is another line.
And this is the last line.
```

Code block: E.6.3.1.3

Exercise 6.3.2: Copying a File

Create a program that reads a given file and creates a new file with its content.

Instructions:

1. Read the provided "source.txt" file.
2. Create a new file called "destination.txt" and write the content of "source.txt" into it.

Solution:

```python
source_filename = "source.txt"
destination_filename = "destination.txt"

with open(source_filename, "r") as source_file:
    content = source_file.read()

    with open(destination_filename, "w") as destination_file:
        destination_file.write(content)

print(f"Content from {source_filename} has been copied to {destination_filename}.")
```

Code block: E.6.3.2.1

Output:

```
Content from source.txt has been copied to destination.txt.
```

Code block: E.6.3.2.2

Exercise 6.3.3: Reading a Specific Line

Create a program that reads a given file and prints the content of a specific line number.

Instructions:

1. Read the provided "lines.txt" file.
2. Prompt the user to enter a line number.
3. Print the content of the specified line.

Solution:

```python
filename = "lines.txt"

with open(filename, "r") as f:
    lines = f.readlines()

line_number = int(input("Enter the line number: "))
if 0 < line_number <= len(lines):
    print(f"Line {line_number}: {lines[line_number - 1].strip()}")
else:
    print("Invalid line number.")
```

Code block: E.6.3.3.1

Output (example):

```
Enter the line number: 2
Line 2: This is the second line.
```

Code block: E.6.3.3.2

The "lines.txt" file has the following content:

```
This is the first line.
This is the second line.
This is the third line.
This is the fourth line.
```

Code block. E 6.3.3.3

6.4: Handling Exceptions in File Operations

When working with files, it is crucial to handle exceptions that may occur during file operations. An exception is an event that occurs when a runtime error is encountered, causing the program to stop executing. By handling exceptions, you can ensure that your program continues to run smoothly even if an error occurs.

There are many types of exceptions that you may encounter when working with files. Some of the most common include file not found, access denied, and invalid file format. Each of these exceptions requires a different approach to handling, and it is essential to understand how to handle each type of exception properly.

One way to handle exceptions is to use a try-catch block. This block of code allows you to attempt an operation and catch any exceptions that may occur. By catching the exception, you can handle it appropriately, such as displaying an error message or attempting to recover from the error.

Another way to handle exceptions is to use a finally block. This block of code is executed regardless of whether an exception occurs or not. This is useful for closing files or freeing up resources, ensuring that your program is still running efficiently.

In addition to handling exceptions, it is also essential to ensure that your program is secure when working with files. This includes validating user input, ensuring that files are not overwritten accidentally, and preventing unauthorized access to files. By taking these steps, you can ensure that your program is robust and secure when working with files.

Python uses the **try**, **except**, and **finally** blocks to handle exceptions in file operations. Let's explore these concepts in detail.

1. **try**: The **try** block contains the code that might raise an exception. If an exception occurs in the **try** block, the execution moves to the appropriate **except** block.
2. **except**: The **except** block contains the code that will execute when an exception is raised in the **try** block. You can catch specific exception types, allowing you to handle different exceptions with different code. If you don't specify an exception type, the **except** block will catch all exceptions.
3. **finally**: The **finally** block contains code that will always execute, regardless of whether an exception occurred or not. This block is often used for clean-up tasks, such as closing a file.

Here's an example of handling exceptions in file operations:

```python
filename = "nonexistent_file.txt"

try:
    with open(filename, "r") as file:
        content = file.read()
except FileNotFoundError:
    print(f"The file '{filename}' does not exist.")
except Exception as e:
    print(f"An error occurred while reading the file: {e}")
else:
    print("The file was read successfully.")
finally:
    print("This message will always be printed.")
```

Code block: 6.9

In this example, if the file does not exist, a **FileNotFoundError** exception will be raised, and the corresponding **except** block will execute. If any other exception occurs, the general **except** block with **Exception as e** will execute. If no exception occurs, the **else** block will execute. The **finally** block will always execute, regardless of whether an exception occurred or not.

When writing code, it's important to think not only about the happy path, but also about the different scenarios that can occur, such as unexpected errors or exceptions. One area where this is particularly important is when dealing with file operations. By taking the time to consider and handle the possible exceptions that might occur when reading or writing files, you can make your programs more robust and resilient to errors.

For example, what if the file you're trying to open doesn't exist, or you don't have the necessary permissions to access it? What if the file is being used by another process, or the disk is full? These are all potential scenarios that could cause your program to crash or behave unexpectedly if not handled properly.

By anticipating and handling these exceptions appropriately, you can ensure a smooth and error-free user experience. This might involve displaying helpful error messages to the user, logging errors for debugging purposes, or taking other actions to gracefully recover from the error.

So, don't forget to take the time to think about exception handling when working with files. It might take a little extra effort up front, but it will pay off in the long run by making your programs more reliable and user-friendly.

Exercise 6.4.1: Handling FileNotFoundError

In this exercise, you will handle a **FileNotFoundError** when trying to read a non-existent file.

Instructions:

1. Write a Python program that tries to read a file named "nonexistent_file.txt".
2. Handle the **FileNotFoundError** exception and print a message to inform the user that the file does not exist.

Solution:

```python
filename = "nonexistent_file.txt"

try:
    with open(filename, "r") as file:
        content = file.read()
except FileNotFoundError:
    print(f"The file '{filename}' does not exist.")
```

Code block: E.6.4.1.1

Output:

```
The file 'nonexistent_file.txt' does not exist.
```

Code block: E.6.4.1.2

Exercise 6.4.2: Handling PermissionError

In this exercise, you will handle a **PermissionError** when trying to write to a read-only file.

Instructions:

1. Create a read-only file named "readonly_file.txt" and write some content to it.
2. Write a Python program that tries to append new content to the read-only file.
3. Handle the **PermissionError** exception and print a message to inform the user that the file is read-only.

Solution:

```
filename = "readonly_file.txt"

try:
    with open(filename, "a") as file:
        file.write("Appending new content")
except PermissionError:
    print(f"Cannot write to the file '{filename}' as it is read-only.")
```

Code block: E.6.4.2.1

Output:

```
Cannot write to the file 'readonly_file.txt' as it is read-only.
```

Code block: E.6.4.2.2

Exercise 6.4.3: Using Finally Block

In this exercise, you will use the **finally** block to ensure that a file is closed after reading its content.

Instructions:

1. Create a file named "my_file.txt" and write some content to it.
2. Write a Python program that tries to read the content of the file.
3. Use the **finally** block to close the file, regardless of whether an exception occurred or not.

Solution:

```
filename = "my_file.txt"

try:
    file = open(filename, "r")
    content = file.read()
    print(content)
except Exception as e:
    print(f"An error occurred while reading the file: {e}")
finally:
    file.close()
    print("The file was closed.")
```

Code block: E.6.4.3.1

Output:

```
[Content of my_file.txt]
The file was closed.
```

Code block: E.6.4.3.2

Congratulations on completing Chapter 6 on Working with Files! In this chapter, we explored the basics of handling files in Python, including opening and closing files, reading and writing file content, understanding file modes, and handling exceptions in file operations.

By now, you should have a solid understanding of how to work with files in Python. You've learned how to handle common exceptions that might occur during file operations, such as **FileNotFoundError** and **PermissionError**. These skills are essential for any Python developer, as handling files is a common task in many programming projects.

As you progress in your Python journey, you may come across more advanced file handling concepts, like working with binary files or handling larger files efficiently using buffering. Keep learning and practicing, and don't forget to refer back to this chapter whenever you need a refresher on file handling in Python.

CHAPTER 7: Modules and Packages

In this chapter, we will explore the fascinating world of modules and packages in Python. These two concepts are fundamental to any programming language, as they allow for the organization and reuse of code in a structured and systematic way.

Python is particularly known for its rich standard library, which contains a plethora of built-in modules that provide a wide range of functionality. Some of the most commonly used modules include "os" for operating system interactions, "math" for mathematical operations, and "random" for generating random numbers. Additionally, there are numerous third-party packages available for various purposes, which can be easily installed using tools such as pip.

By understanding how to work with modules and packages, you will be able to write more efficient and modular code, saving you time and effort in the long run. You will also be able to take advantage of the vast array of pre-existing functionality available in the Python ecosystem, which can greatly benefit your projects and workflow. So let's dive in and discover the power of modules and packages in Python!

7.1: Importing Modules

Python modules are files that contain Python code. They are used to organize your code into reusable components, making it easier to maintain and understand. The most common way to use a module is to import it into your script or another module. This allows you to access the functions, classes, and variables defined in the imported module.

To import a module in Python, you can use the **import** statement, followed by the name of the module. For example, if you want to import the built-in **math** module, you can do this:

```
import math
```

Code block. 7.1

Once you have imported a module, you can access its functions, classes, and variables using the dot (.) notation. Here's an example of using the **sqrt** function from the **math** module:

```python
import math

square_root = math.sqrt(16)
print(square_root)  # Output: 4.0
```

Code block: 7.2

You can also use the **from** keyword to import specific functions, classes, or variables from a module. This allows you to access them directly, without needing to use the dot notation. Here's an example of importing the **sqrt** function from the **math** module:

```python
from math import sqrt

square_root = sqrt(16)
print(square_root)  # Output: 4.0
```

Code block: 7.3

In some cases, you may want to import a module or a specific function, class, or variable with an alias. You can use the **as** keyword for this purpose. This can be especially helpful when working with modules that have long or complicated names. Here's an example of importing the **math** module with an alias:

```python
import math as m

square_root = m.sqrt(16)
print(square_root)  # Output: 4.0
```

Code block: 7.4

When it comes to importing modules in Python, it is important to keep in mind that there are different ways to approach it. Although it may be tempting to import an entire module, it is generally considered best practice to only import the specific functions, classes, or variables that you need. Not only can this make your code more efficient by reducing the amount of memory used, but it also makes your code more readable by clearly indicating which parts of the module are being used.

Moving on to the next topics, there is much more to discuss about modules and packages in Python. In addition to importing modules, you can also create and organize your own modules and packages to better structure your code. Moreover, you may find yourself working with third-party packages that provide additional functionality beyond what is included in the standard library. By learning how to work with modules and packages, you can greatly improve the organization and efficiency of your Python code.

Exercise 7.1.1: Random Number Generator

In this exercise, you will generate a random integer between 1 and 100 using the **random** module.

Instructions:

1. Import the **random** module.
2. Generate a random integer between 1 and 100 using the **randint** function.
3. Print the generated random integer.

Solution:

```
import random

random_integer = random.randint(1, 100)
print(random_integer)
```

Code block: 7.1.1.1

Output: (Note that the output will vary since it's a random number)

```
42
```

Code block: 7.1.1.2

Exercise 7.1.2: Current Date and Time

In this exercise, you will print the current date and time using the **datetime** module.

Instructions:

1. Import the **datetime** module.
2. Get the current date and time using the **datetime.now()** function.
3. Print the current date and time.

Solution:

```
import datetime

current_date_time = datetime.datetime.now()
print(current_date_time)
```

Code block: 7.1.2.1

Output: (Note that the output will vary depending on the current date and time)

```
2023-03-29 12:34:56.789012
```

Code block: 7.1.2.2

Exercise 7.1.3: Calculate the Area of a Circle

In this exercise, you will calculate the area of a circle with a given radius using the **pi** constant from the **math** module.

Instructions:

1. Import the **pi** constant from the **math** module.
2. Define a variable **radius** and assign it a value, for example, 5.
3. Calculate the area of the circle using the formula **area = pi * radius * radius**.
4. Print the area of the circle.

Solution:

```python
from math import pi

radius = 5
area = pi * radius * radius
print(area)
```

Code block: 7.1.3.1

Output:

```
78.53981633974483
```

Code block: 7.1.3.2

7.2: Standard Library Modules

In this section, we will delve into the Python Standard Library, which is a set of pre-installed modules that offer a wide range of functionalities. These modules are useful for performing various tasks without the need for third-party libraries. They can be used to work with the file system, interact with the internet, manipulate data, and much more.

The Python Standard Library is an essential tool for any Python programmer. It includes modules for working with regular expressions, cryptography, network programming, and more. One of the most commonly used modules is the os module, which provides a way to interact with the file system. You can use this module to create, delete, or modify files and directories, as well as to navigate the file system.

Another commonly used module is the urllib module, which provides a way to interact with the internet. You can use this module to download web pages, send HTTP requests, and more. The urllib module is particularly useful for web scraping and data analysis tasks.

In addition to these commonly used modules, the Python Standard Library includes modules for working with dates and times, parsing XML, and more. These modules can be used to perform a wide range of tasks, from simple file management to complex data analysis.

Here are a few essential standard library modules that you may find useful:

7.2.1: os

The **os** module provides a way to interact with the operating system. It allows you to perform file and directory operations, such as creating, renaming, or deleting files and directories. Additionally, you can retrieve information about the system, like the environment variables or the current working directory.

Example:

```python
import os

# Get the current working directory
current_directory = os.getcwd()
print(current_directory)
```

Code block: 7.5

7.2.2: sys

The **sys** module provides access to some variables used or maintained by the interpreter and functions that interact with the interpreter. For example, you can use it to access command-line arguments or manipulate the Python path.

Example:

```python
import sys

# Print the Python version
print(sys.version)
```

Code block: 7.6

7.2.3: re

The **re** module provides support for regular expressions, which are a powerful tool for text processing. You can use them to search, match, or substitute specific patterns in strings.

Example:

```python
import re

text = "Hello, my name is John Doe"
pattern = r"\b\w{4}\b"

four_letter_words = re.findall(pattern, text)
print(four_letter_words)
```

Code block: 7.7

7.2.4: json

The **json** module allows you to work with JSON data by encoding and decoding JSON strings. You can use this module to read and write JSON data to and from files, as well as to convert JSON data to Python objects and vice versa.

Example:

```python
import json

data = {
    "name": "John",
    "age": 30,
    "city": "New York"
}

# Convert the Python dictionary to a JSON string
json_data = json.dumps(data)
print(json_data)
```

Code block: 7.8

7.2.5: urllib

The **urllib** module is a part of Python's standard library and is used for working with URLs. It provides various functions to interact with URLs and fetch data from the internet. The **urllib** module is further divided into several sub-modules, such as **urllib.request**, **urllib.parse**, and **urllib.error**.

Here's a brief explanation of the most commonly used sub-modules:

- **urllib.request**: This sub-module provides functions to open and read URLs. The most common method is **urlopen**, which can be used to fetch data from a URL.

Example:

```
import urllib.request

url = "https://www.example.com"
response = urllib.request.urlopen(url)
content = response.read()

print(content)
```

Code block 7.9

- **urllib.parse**: This sub-module contains functions to manipulate and parse URLs, such as splitting a URL into its components or encoding/decoding query parameters.

Example:

```
from urllib.parse import urlparse, urlencode

url = "https://www.example.com/search?q=python+programming"

# Parse the URL into components
parsed_url = urlparse(url)
print(parsed_url)

# Encode query parameters
query_params = {"q": "python programming", "page": 2}
encoded_params = urlencode(query_params)
print(encoded_params)
```

Code block 7.10

- **urllib.error**: This sub-module defines exception classes for handling errors that may occur during URL handling, such as HTTP errors or network-related issues. Some common exceptions are **URLError** and **HTTPError**.

Example:

```
import urllib.request
from urllib.error import URLError, HTTPError

url = "https://www.nonexistentwebsite.com"

try:
    response = urllib.request.urlopen(url)
except HTTPError as e:
    print(f"HTTP error occurred: {e}")
except URLError as e:
    print(f"URL error occurred: {e}")
```

Code block: 7.11

These sub-modules combined offer a powerful way to interact with the internet and manipulate URLs. However, in many cases, developers prefer to use the third-party library **requests** for making HTTP requests, as it offers a more user-friendly API and additional features. If you're interested, you can learn more about the **requests** library here: https://docs.python-requests.org/en/master/

These are just a few examples of the many standard library modules available in Python. To explore more modules and learn about their functionalities, refer to the Python documentation: https://docs.python.org/3/library/

Exercise 7.2.1: Create a Simple Module

In this exercise, you will create a simple module that contains a function to calculate the area of a rectangle.

Instructions:

1. Create a new Python file called **geometry.py**.
2. Define a function named **rectangle_area** that takes two arguments: **length** and **width**.
3. The function should return the product of **length** and **width**.
4. Import the **geometry** module in another Python script and use the **rectangle_area** function.

Solution:

Create **geometry.py**:

```python
def rectangle_area(length, width):
    return length * width
```

Code block: 7.2.1.1

In another Python script, import the **geometry** module and use the **rectangle_area** function:

```python
import geometry

area = geometry.rectangle_area(5, 10)
print(f"Area of the rectangle: {area}")
```

Code block: 7.2.1.2

Output:

```
Area of the rectangle: 50
```

Code block: 7.2.1.3

Exercise 7.2.2: Create a Custom Text Manipulation Module

Create a custom module called **text_manipulation** that contains functions for converting a string to uppercase, lowercase, and title case.

Instructions:

1. Create a Python file called **text_manipulation.py**.

2. Define three functions: **to_upper**, **to_lower**, and **to_title**.
3. Each function should take a single argument, a string, and return the modified string.
4. Import the **text_manipulation** module in another Python script and use the functions.

Solution:

Create **text_manipulation.py**:

```python
def to_upper(text):
    return text.upper()

def to_lower(text):
    return text.lower()

def to_title(text):
    return text.title()
```

Code block: 7.2.2.1

In another Python script, import the **text_manipulation** module and use the functions:

```python
import text_manipulation

text = "this is a sample text"

upper_text = text_manipulation.to_upper(text)
print(f"Uppercase: {upper_text}")

lower_text = text_manipulation.to_lower(text)
print(f"Lowercase: {lower_text}")

title_text = text_manipulation.to_title(text)
print(f"Title case: {title_text}")
```

Code block: 7.2.2.2

Output:

```
Uppercase: THIS IS A SAMPLE TEXT
Lowercase: this is a sample text
Title case: This Is A Sample Text
```

Code block: 7.2.2.3

Exercise 7.2.3: Create a Module with Constants

In this exercise, you will create a module called **constants** that contains a few mathematical constants.

Instructions:

1. Create a Python file called **constants.py**.
2. Define variables for the following constants: **PI**, **E**, and **GOLDEN_RATIO**.
3. Import the **constants** module in another Python script and use the constants.

Solution:

Create **constants.py**:

```
PI = 3.141592653589793
E = 2.718281828459045
GOLDEN_RATIO = 1.618033988749895
```

Code block: 7.2.3.1

In another Python script, import the **constants** module and use the constants:

```
import constants

print(f"PI: {constants.PI}")
print(f"E: {constants.E}")
print(f"Golden Ratio: {constants.GOLDEN_RATIO}")
```

Code block: 7.2.3.2

Output:

```
PI: 3.141592653589793
E: 2.718281828459045
Golden Ratio: 1.
```

Code block: 7.2.3.3

7.3: Creating Your Own Modules

In this section, we will discuss creating your own Python packages. A package is a collection of Python modules that are organized in a directory hierarchy. By creating your own packages, you can structure your code in a more organized and modular way, making it easier to maintain and share.

When creating your own package, it is important to consider the overall structure and organization of your modules. You may want to group related modules together into subpackages, or create a separate package for each major component of your code. This can help to keep your code organized and easy to navigate.

Another important consideration when creating a package is how to properly document your code. This can include writing docstrings for your modules and functions, as well as creating a README file that explains how to use your package and any dependencies that it may have.

Once you have created your package, you can share it with others by uploading it to the Python Package Index (PyPI) or by making it available on GitHub. This can be a great way to contribute to the Python community and to showcase your coding skills.

Overall, creating your own Python packages can be a valuable skill for any Python developer. By organizing your code in a more modular and maintainable way, you can improve the quality and reliability of your code, making it easier to build and maintain complex applications.

7.3.1: To create a Python package, follow these steps:

1. **Create a directory**: Start by creating a new directory for your package. The directory's name should be descriptive of the package's functionality. For example, if you're creating a package for handling dates and times, you might name the directory **datetime_utils**.
2. **Add an __init__.py file**: Inside the newly created directory, create a file named **__init__.py**. This file is required for Python to treat the directory as a package. The **__init__.py** file can be empty or contain package-level initialization code.
3. **Add modules**: Inside the package directory, create Python files (with a **.py** extension) for each module you want to include in your package. These files will contain the functions, classes, and variables that you want to make available to users of your package.
4. **Importing and using your package**: To use your package in a Python script or another package, simply import it using the **import** statement. You can use the package name

and the module name separated by a dot to import specific modules or objects from your package.

For example, let's create a package called **datetime_utils** that contains two modules: **date_operations** and **time_operations**.

1. Create a directory named **datetime_utils**.
2. Inside the **datetime_utils** directory, create an empty file named **__init__.py**.
3. Create two Python files inside the **datetime_utils** directory: **date_operations.py** and **time_operations.py**.

date_operations.py:

```python
def days_between_dates(date1, date2):
    delta = date2 - date1
    return delta.days
```

Code block: 7.11

time_operations.py:

```python
def seconds_between_times(time1, time2):
    delta = time2 - time1
    return delta.total_seconds()
```

Code block: 7.12

1. In another Python script, import and use the **datetime_utils** package:

```
from datetime import datetime
from datetime_utils import date_operations, time_operations

date1 = datetime(2022, 1, 1)
date2 = datetime(2022, 1, 10)

days = date_operations.days_between_dates(date1, date2)
print(f"Days between dates: {days}")

time1 = datetime(2022, 1, 1, 12, 0, 0)
time2 = datetime(2022, 1, 1, 14, 30, 0)

seconds = time_operations.seconds_between_times(time1, time2)
print(f"Seconds between times: {seconds}")
```

Code block: 7.13

Output:

```
Days between dates: 9
Seconds between times: 9000.0
```

Code block: 7.14

This is a basic example of creating a Python package. While this example is simple, it is important to note that creating more complex packages with nested directories and multiple modules is also possible. For instance, a package could contain sub-packages that correspond to different sections of an application, or modules that are designed to work together in a particular way. Additionally, there are many different ways that packages can be used, such as for creating reusable code libraries, distributing code to others, or simply for organizing code within a larger project. Therefore, it is important to consider the specific needs of your project when deciding how to structure your package.

Exercise 7.3.1: Creating a Simple Math Package

Create a package called **simple_math** that contains two modules: **basic_operations** and **advanced_operations**.

Instructions:

1. Create a directory named **simple_math** and add an empty **__init__.py** file.
2. Create a **basic_operations.py** module that contains the following functions: **add**, **subtract**, **multiply**, and **divide**.
3. Create an **advanced_operations.py** module that contains the following functions: **power** and **sqrt** (square root).
4. In a separate Python script, import and use the **simple_math** package to perform some calculations.

Solution:

simple_math/basic_operations.py:

```python
def add(x, y):
    return x + y

def subtract(x, y):
    return x - y

def multiply(x, y):
    return x * y

def divide(x, y):
    if y == 0:
        raise ValueError("Division by zero is not allowed")
    return x / y
```

Code block: E.7.3.1.1

simple_math/advanced_operations.py:

```python
def power(x, y):
    return x ** y

def sqrt(x):
    if x < 0:
        raise ValueError("Square root of a negative number is not allowed")
    return x ** 0.5
```

Code block: E.7.3.1.2

main.py:

```python
from simple_math import basic_operations, advanced_operations

print("Addition:", basic_operations.add(5, 3))
print("Subtraction:", basic_operations.subtract(5, 3))
print("Multiplication:", basic_operations.multiply(5, 3))
print("Division:", basic_operations.divide(5, 3))
print("Power:", advanced_operations.power(5, 3))
print("Square root:", advanced_operations.sqrt(9))
```

Code block: E.7.3.1.3

Output:

```
Addition: 8
Subtraction: 2
Multiplication: 15
Division: 1.6666666666666667
Power: 125
Square root: 3.0
```

Code block: E.7.3.1.4

Exercise 7.3.2: Creating a Text Processing Package

Description: Create a package called **text_processing** that contains a module called **text_utils** with the following functions: **count_words**, **count_characters**, and **average_word_length**.

Instructions:

1. Create a directory named **text_processing** and add an empty **__init__.py** file.
2. Create a **text_utils.py** module with the specified functions.
3. In a separate Python script, import and use the **text_processing** package to process a sample text.

Solution:

text_processing/text_utils.py:

```python
def count_words(text):
    return len(text.split())

def count_characters(text):
    return len(text)

def average_word_length(text):
    words = text.split()
    total_characters = sum(len(word) for word in words)
    return total_characters / len(words)
```

Code block: E.7.3.2.1

main.py:

```python
from text_processing import text_utils

sample_text = "This is a sample text for the text_processing package."

print("Word count:", text_utils.count_words(sample_text))
print("Character count:", text_utils.count_characters(sample_text))
print("Average word length:", text_utils.average_word_length(sample_text))
```

Code block: E.7.3.2.2

Output:

```
Word count: 9
Character count: 50
Average word length: 4.555555555555555
```

Code block: E.7.3.2.3

Exercise 7.3.3: Creating a Geometry Package

Create a package called **geometry** that contains a module called **area_calculations** with the following functions: **rectangle_area**, **triangle_area**, and **circle_area**.

Instructions:

1. Create a directory named **geometry** and add an empty **__init__.py** file.
2. Create an **area_calculations.py** module with the specified functions.
3. In a separate Python script, import and use the **geometry** package to calculate the areas of different shapes.

Solution:

geometry/area_calculations.py:

```python
import math

def rectangle_area(width, height):
    return width * height

def triangle_area(base, height):
    return 0.5 * base * height

def circle_area(radius):
    return math.pi * radius * radius
```

Code block: E.7.3.3.1

main.py:

```python
from geometry import area_calculations

print("Rectangle area:", area_calculations.rectangle_area(5, 3))
print("Triangle area:", area_calculations.triangle_area(5, 3))
print("Circle area:", area_calculations.circle_area(5))
```

Code block: E.7.3.3.2

Output:

```
Rectangle area: 15
Triangle area: 7.5
Circle area: 78.53981633974483
```

Code block: E.7.3.3.3

7.4 Python Packages

In the previous sections, we discussed modules and how to create and use them. In addition to being a powerful tool for code organization, modules also allow for code reuse, simplifying development and maintenance tasks.

In this section, we'll dive into Python packages, which are a way of organizing related modules in a hierarchical structure. Packages provide yet another level of organization within a codebase, making it easy to group and manage a large number of modules. By breaking up code into smaller, more easily manageable pieces, packages help developers maintain order and clarity within their projects.

Furthermore, packages can be shared between projects, making them an ideal tool for promoting code reuse across an entire organization.

A Python package is simply a directory that contains a collection of modules and a special file called **__init__.py**. The presence of this file tells Python that the directory should be treated as a package. The **__init__.py** file can be empty or contain initialization code for your package.

Let's understand packages with an easy explanation:

7.4.1: Creating a package:

To create a package, first, create a directory with a suitable name. Then, create an **__init__.py** file inside the directory.

For example, let's create a package called **vehicles**. Create a directory named **vehicles** and add an empty **__init__.py** file to it.

7.4.2: Adding modules to a package:

You can add modules to the package by simply creating **.py** files within the package directory.

For example, let's add two modules to our **vehicles** package: **cars.py** and **trucks.py**.

7.4.3: Importing and using packages:

To use a package, simply use the **import** statement followed by the package name and the module name, separated by a dot.

For example, to use the **cars** module from the **vehicles** package, you would write **import vehicles.cars**. You can also use the **from ... import ...** statement to import specific functions or classes.

Here's a brief example to demonstrate packages:

vehicles/__init__.py:

```
# This can be empty or contain package-level initialization code.
```

Code block: 7.15

vehicles/cars.py:

```python
def car_description(make, model):
    return f"{make} {model}"
```

vehicles/trucks.py:

```python
def truck_description(make, model, bed_size):
    return f"{make} {model} with a {bed_size} bed"
```

main.py:

```python
from vehicles.cars import car_description
from vehicles.trucks import truck_description

print(car_description("Toyota", "Camry"))
print(truck_description("Ford", "F-150", "6.5 ft"))
```

Output:

```
Toyota Camry
Ford F-150 with a 6.5 ft bed
```

Python packages provide an efficient way of organizing related modules into a hierarchical structure, enabling developers to manage and maintain larger projects with ease. This feature is especially useful when working on complex software projects with a lot of code.

Packages are directories that contain one or more python modules, with an **__init__.py** file defining the package. The **__init__.py** file is executed when the package is imported, which allows for customization of the package's behavior. This file can contain variables, functions, or classes that are used across the modules in the package.

By grouping related modules together into a package, it becomes easier to manage dependencies between them. This promotes code reuse and makes it easier for others to understand the codebase. Additionally, packages can be distributed as standalone units, making them easy to share and reuse across multiple projects.

Overall, using packages in Python is an excellent way to keep your code organized and maintainable, making it easier to work on larger projects and collaborate with others. Remember, packages are a fundamental feature of the Python language, so it's essential to learn how to use them effectively.

Exercise 7.4.1: Creating and using a simple package

In this exercise, you will create a package named **shapes** containing two modules: **rectangle.py** and **circle.py**. Each module should contain functions to calculate the area and perimeter of the respective shape. Finally, you will import and use these functions in a script called **main.py**.

Instructions:

1. Create a package named **shapes** with an empty **__init__.py** file.
2. Create a module **rectangle.py** inside the **shapes** package containing the following functions:
    - **area(width, height)**: Returns the area of a rectangle.
    - **perimeter(width, height)**: Returns the perimeter of a rectangle.
3. Create a module **circle.py** inside the **shapes** package containing the following functions:
    - **area(radius)**: Returns the area of a circle.
    - **circumference(radius)**: Returns the circumference of a circle.
4. In **main.py**, import and use the functions from both modules to calculate the area and perimeter of a rectangle with width 5 and height 7, and the area and circumference of a circle with radius 4.

Solution:

shapes/__init__.py:

```python
# This can be empty or contain package-level initialization code.
```

Code block: E.7.4.1.1

shapes/rectangle.py:

```python
def area(width, height):
    return width * height

def perimeter(width, height):
    return 2 * (width + height)
```

Code block: E.7.4.1.2

shapes/circle.py:

```python
import math

def area(radius):
    return math.pi * radius ** 2

def circumference(radius):
    return 2 * math.pi * radius
```

Code block: E.7.4.1.3

main.py:

```
from shapes.rectangle import area as rect_area, perimeter as rect_perimeter
from shapes.circle import area as circle_area, circumference as circle_circumfer
ence

width = 5
height = 7
radius = 4

print(f"Rectangle area: {rect_area(width, height)}")
print(f"Rectangle perimeter: {rect_perimeter(width, height)}")
print(f"Circle area: {circle_area(radius)}")
print(f"Circle circumference: {circle_circumference(radius)}")
```

Code block: E.7.4.1.4

Output:

```
Rectangle area: 35
Rectangle perimeter: 24
Circle area: 50.26548245743669
Circle circumference: 25.132741228718345
```

Code block: E.7.4.1.5

Exercise 7.4.2: Creating a Package

In this exercise, you will create a simple package named **my_math** containing two modules, **addition** and **multiplication**. Each module will have functions to perform basic arithmetic operations.

Instructions:

1. Create a folder named **my_math** to serve as your package.

2. Inside the **my_math** folder, create two Python files named **addition.py** and **multiplication.py**.
3. In **addition.py**, define a function **add(a, b)** that returns the sum of the two input numbers.
4. In **multiplication.py**, define a function **multiply(a, b)** that returns the product of the two input numbers.
5. In the main script, import and use both modules to perform addition and multiplication.

Solution:

```python
# my_math/addition.py
def add(a, b):
    return a + b
```

Code block: E.7.4.2.1

```python
# my_math/multiplication.py
def multiply(a, b):
    return a * b
```

Code block: E.7.4.2.2

```python
# main.py
from my_math.addition import add
from my_math.multiplication import multiply

a = 5
b = 3

sum_result = add(a, b)
product_result = multiply(a, b)

print(f"{a} + {b} = {sum_result}")
print(f"{a} * {b} = {product_result}")
```

Code block: E.7.4.2.3

Output:

```
5 + 3 = 8
5 * 3 = 15
```

Code block: E.7.4.2.4

Exercise 7.4.3: Using third-party packages

In this exercise, you will install and use a third-party package to generate random names. You will create a script that generates and prints a random name using the **names** package.

Instructions:

1. Install the **names** package using **pip install names**.
2. Create a script **random_name.py** that imports the **names** package.
3. Use the **names.get_full_name()** function to generate a random full name.
4. Print the random full name.

Solution:

```
# random_name.py
import names

random_full_name = names.get_full_name()
print(f"Random full name: {random_full_name}")
```

Code block: E.7.4.3.1

Output (sample):

```
Random full name: John Smith
```

Code block: E.7.4.3.2

Note: The output will vary each time you run the script since it generates a random name.

Congratulations on completing Chapter 7! In this chapter, you learned about Python modules and packages, essential tools for organizing and structuring your code.

You started by understanding how to import modules and use the functions they provide. Next, you explored some of the standard library modules, such as **os**, **random**, **math**, and **urllib**, which provide useful functionalities in different areas.

We then moved on to creating your own modules, allowing you to reuse and share your code more easily. Finally, you learned about packages, which are a way to group related modules together, creating a more structured and organized codebase.

As you continue to work on more complex projects, you'll find that modules and packages are indispensable for managing code, avoiding duplication, and improving maintainability. Keep practicing, and don't be afraid to explore other standard library modules and third-party packages to help you accomplish your tasks more efficiently.

CHAPTER 8: Object-Oriented Programming

Welcome to Chapter 8! In this chapter, we'll dive into the world of Object-Oriented Programming (OOP). OOP is a programming paradigm that allows you to create reusable, modular code by modeling real-world entities as software objects.

Python is an ideal language for OOP, as it fully supports OOP concepts and has a wide range of libraries and frameworks available for implementing OOP. By learning OOP in Python, you'll gain a deeper understanding of programming concepts and be able to create more efficient and effective code.

Additionally, OOP is a widely used programming paradigm in many industries, including software development, artificial intelligence, and web development. By mastering OOP in Python, you'll be setting yourself up for success in a variety of programming fields.

8.1 Classes and Objects

In object-oriented programming, the main concepts are classes and objects. A class is a blueprint for creating objects, which are instances of the class. Classes define the properties (attributes) and behavior (methods) of the objects they represent.

Let's start with a simple example. Consider a class named **Dog**. The **Dog** class can have attributes like **name**, **breed**, and **age**. It can also have methods like **bark()** and **sit()**.

To define a class in Python, you use the **class** keyword:

```
class Dog:
    pass
```

Code block: 8.1

The **pass** keyword is a placeholder that does nothing, but it allows the class definition to be syntactically correct.

Now that we have our **Dog** class, we can create objects (instances) of the class:

```
dog1 = Dog()
dog2 = Dog()
```

Code block: 8.2

Here, **dog1** and **dog2** are two different objects of the **Dog** class. They are separate instances, so we can assign different attributes to them:

```
dog1.name = "Buddy"
dog1.breed = "Golden Retriever"
dog1.age = 3

dog2.name = "Max"
dog2.breed = "Labrador"
dog2.age = 5
```

Code block: 8.3

Now, let's add some methods to our **Dog** class:

```
class Dog:
    def bark(self):
        print("Woof!")

    def sit(self):
        print(f"{self.name} sits.")
```

Code block 8.4

The **self** parameter in the method definition is a reference to the instance of the class. It allows you to access the object's attributes and call other methods within the class.

Now, we can create instances of our updated **Dog** class and call their methods:

```
dog1 = Dog()
dog1.name = "Buddy"
dog1.bark()    # Output: Woof!
dog1.sit()     # Output: Buddy sits.

dog2 = Dog()
dog2.name = "Max"
dog2.bark()    # Output: Woof!
dog2.sit()     # Output: Max sits.
```

Code block 8.5

In this section, we have learned the basics of defining classes and creating objects in Python. However, it is important to note that there are many different types of classes that can be defined, each with their own unique characteristics and behaviors.

For example, some classes may require additional parameters to be defined in their constructors, while others may inherit properties and methods from parent classes. Additionally, the concept of encapsulation is a fundamental aspect of object-oriented programming, which involves restricting access to certain properties and methods within a class in order to maintain data integrity and prevent unintended modifications.

As we move forward in this book, we will explore these more advanced OOP concepts in greater detail, building upon the foundation that we have established in this section.

Exercise 8.1.1: Define a Car class

In this exercise, you will define a **Car** class with two attributes **make** and **model**, and a method **honk()** that prints "Beep! Beep!".

Instructions:

1. Define a **Car** class with attributes **make** and **model**.
2. Add a **honk()** method to the **Car** class that prints "Beep! Beep!".
3. Create an instance of the **Car** class, set its **make** and **model** attributes, and call its **honk()** method.

Solution:

```python
class Car:
    def honk(self):
        print("Beep! Beep!")

my_car = Car()
my_car.make = "Toyota"
my_car.model = "Corolla"
my_car.honk()  # Output: Beep! Beep!
```

Block code: E.8.1.1.1

Exercise 8.1.2: Define a Circle class

In this exercise, you will define a **Circle** class with an attribute **radius** and two methods **area()** and **circumference()** that calculate and return the area and circumference of the circle, respectively.

Instructions:

1. Define a **Circle** class with an attribute **radius**.

2. Add an **area()** method that calculates and returns the area of the circle using the formula **area = pi * radius^2**. You can use **math.pi** for the value of pi.
3. Add a **circumference()** method that calculates and returns the circumference of the circle using the formula **circumference = 2 * pi * radius**.
4. Create an instance of the **Circle** class, set its **radius** attribute, and call its **area()** and **circumference()** methods.

Solution:

```
import math

class Circle:
    def area(self):
        return math.pi * self.radius ** 2

    def circumference(self):
        return 2 * math.pi * self.radius

my_circle = Circle()
my_circle.radius = 5
print(my_circle.area())            # Output: 78.53981633974483
print(my_circle.circumference())   # Output: 31.41592653589793
```

Block code: E.8.1.2.1

Exercise 8.1.3: Define a BankAccount class

In this exercise, you will define a **BankAccount** class with two attributes **account_number** and **balance**, and two methods **deposit(amount)** and **withdraw(amount)** for depositing and withdrawing money.

Instructions:

1. Define a **BankAccount** class with attributes **account_number** and **balance**.
2. Add a **deposit(amount)** method that increases the balance by the given amount.
3. Add a **withdraw(amount)** method that decreases the balance by the given amount, but only if there's enough balance to cover the withdrawal.

4. Create an instance of the **BankAccount** class, set its **account_number** and **balance** attributes, and call its **deposit()** and **withdraw()** methods.

Solution:

```python
class BankAccount:
    def deposit(self, amount):
        self.balance += amount

    def withdraw(self, amount):
        if amount <= self.balance:
            self.balance -= amount
        else:
            print("Insufficient balance")

my_account = BankAccount()
my_account.account_number = "123456789"
my_account.balance = 500
my_account.deposit(300)
print(my_account.balance)   # Output: 800
my_account.withdraw(200)
print(my_account.balance)   # Output: 600
my_account.withdraw(800)    # Output: Insufficient balance
```

Block code: E.8.1.3.1

8.2: Attributes and Methods

In object-oriented programming (OOP), a class can have two types of members: attributes and methods. Attributes are variables that store data specific to an object, while methods are functions that define the behavior of the class and its objects. In this section, we'll dive deeper into attributes and methods and how to use them effectively in Python.

Attributes are the building blocks of an object in a class. They store information about the state of the object and can be accessed and modified by the methods of the class. For example, a class that represents a car may have attributes such as make, model, and year. These attributes can be set when the object is created and modified throughout the life of the object.

Methods, on the other hand, define the behavior of the class and its objects. They can perform operations on the attributes of the object, or they can interact with other objects in the program. For example, a class that represents a car may have methods such as start_engine, stop_engine, and accelerate. These methods can be called on the object to perform specific actions.

In Python, attributes and methods are defined within the class definition using the keyword "self". The "self" keyword refers to the object that the attribute or method belongs to. When an object is created from a class, it is referred to as an instance of that class. The attributes and methods of the class can be accessed through the instance of the class.

Overall, understanding the difference between attributes and methods is crucial in creating effective and efficient object-oriented programs. By utilizing attributes and methods appropriately, you can create objects that are powerful and flexible, and that can perform a wide range of tasks.

8.2.1: Attributes:

Attributes are variables that belong to an object or a class. There are two types of attributes: instance attributes and class attributes.

Instance attributes: These attributes are specific to an object and are defined within an instance method, usually inside the **__init__** method. Each object of a class has its own set of instance attributes, which means modifying an instance attribute in one object does not affect the other objects of the same class.

```python
class Dog:
    def __init__(self, name, breed):
        self.name = name
        self.breed = breed

dog1 = Dog("Buddy", "Golden Retriever")
dog2 = Dog("Max", "Labrador")
```

Code block: 8.6

In this example, **name** and **breed** are instance attributes.

Class attributes: These attributes are common to all objects of a class and are defined outside of any instance method. Class attributes are useful when you need to store data that should be shared among all instances of a class.

```python
class Dog:
    species = "Canis lupus familiaris"
    
    def __init__(self, name, breed):
        self.name = name
        self.breed = breed

dog1 = Dog("Buddy", "Golden Retriever")
dog2 = Dog("Max", "Labrador")

print(dog1.species)  # Output: Canis lupus familiaris
print(dog2.species)  # Output: Canis lupus familiaris
```

Code block: 8.7

In this example, **species** is a class attribute.

8.2.2: Methods:

Methods are functions that define the behavior of a class and its objects. Similar to attributes, there are two types of methods: instance methods and class methods.

Instance methods: These methods are specific to an object and can access or modify the object's instance attributes. The first parameter of an instance method is always a reference to the object itself, which is typically named **self**.

```python
class Dog:
    def __init__(self, name, breed):
        self.name = name
        self.breed = breed

    def bark(self):
        print(f"{self.name} barks: Woof!")

dog1 = Dog("Buddy", "Golden Retriever")
dog1.bark()   # Output: Buddy barks: Woof!
```

Code block: 8.8

In this example, **bark()** is an instance method.

Class methods: These methods are bound to the class and not the instance of the class. They can't access or modify the instance attributes, but they can access or modify class attributes. To define a class method, use the **@classmethod** decorator and pass the class as the first parameter, typically named **cls**.

```python
class Dog:
    species = "Canis lupus familiaris"

    def __init__(self, name, breed):
        self.name = name
        self.breed = breed

    @classmethod
    def get_species(cls):
        return cls.species

print(Dog.get_species())   # Output: Canis lupus familiaris
```

Code block: 8.9

In this example, **get_species()** is a class method.

In order to effectively use Object-Oriented Programming (OOP) in Python, it is essential to have a solid grasp of attributes and methods. Attributes are essentially variables that are assigned to an object, while methods are functions that are defined within a class and can be called on instances of that class.

By utilizing these concepts, you can create code that is not only more organized, but also more reusable and modular. This can lead to significant advantages when working on larger projects, as it allows for easier maintenance and the ability to quickly implement changes.

Furthermore, by understanding these fundamental principles, you will be better equipped to create more complex and sophisticated programs that can accomplish a wide range of tasks.

Exercise 8.2.1: Car Attributes and Methods

Create a Car class with attributes and methods to describe the car's make, model, and year, as well as a method to display a full description of the car.

Instructions:

1. Create a Car class.
2. Add an **__init__** method to initialize the make, model, and year attributes.
3. Create a method named **description** that returns a string with the car's full description.

Solution:

```python
class Car:
    def __init__(self, make, model, year):
        self.make = make
        self.model = model
        self.year = year

    def description(self):
        return f"{self.year} {self.make} {self.model}"

car1 = Car("Toyota", "Camry", 2021)
print(car1.description())   # Output: 2021 Toyota Camry
```

Code block: E.8.2.1.1

Exercise 8.2.2: Bank Account

Create a BankAccount class with attributes and methods for the account holder's name, balance, and methods to deposit and withdraw money.

Instructions:

1. Create a BankAccount class.
2. Add an __init__ method to initialize the account holder's name and balance (default 0).
3. Create a method named **deposit** to add money to the account balance.
4. Create a method named **withdraw** to subtract money from the account balance. Make sure the withdrawal amount does not exceed the account balance.

Solution:

```python
class BankAccount:
    def __init__(self, name, balance=0):
        self.name = name
        self.balance = balance

    def deposit(self, amount):
        self.balance += amount

    def withdraw(self, amount):
        if amount <= self.balance:
            self.balance -= amount
        else:
            print("Insufficient funds")

account1 = BankAccount("John Doe")
account1.deposit(500)
account1.withdraw(200)
print(account1.balance)   # Output: 300
```

Code block: E.8.2.2.1

Exercise 8.2.3: Circle Class

Description: Create a Circle class with an attribute for the radius and methods to calculate the area and circumference of the circle.

Instructions:

1. Create a Circle class.
2. Add an **__init__** method to initialize the radius attribute.
3. Create a method named **area** to calculate and return the area of the circle (area = π * r^2).
4. Create a method named **circumference** to calculate and return the circumference of the circle (circumference = 2 * π * r).

Solution:

```python
import math

class Circle:
    def __init__(self, radius):
        self.radius = radius

    def area(self):
        return math.pi * (self.radius ** 2)

    def circumference(self):
        return 2 * math.pi * self.radius

circle1 = Circle(5)
print(circle1.area())           # Output: 78.53981633974483
print(circle1.circumference())  # Output: 31.41592653589793
```

Code block: E.8.2.3.1

8.3: Inheritance

Inheritance is one of the most powerful features in object-oriented programming, and it can greatly enhance the efficiency of your code. By allowing one class to inherit the attributes and methods of another class, you can create new classes that are built on top of existing ones, which can save a lot of time and effort.

For example, let's say you have a class that represents a car, with attributes like the make, model, and year, and methods like start_engine and accelerate. Now, let's say you want to create a new class for a specific type of car, like a sports car. Instead of starting from scratch and defining all of the attributes and methods for the sports car, you can simply create a new class that inherits from the car class, and then add or modify the attributes and methods as necessary. This way, you can reuse much of the code that you already wrote for the car class, and only focus on the changes that are specific to the sports car.

In Python, inheritance is implemented by defining a new class that takes the parent (base) class as an argument. The new class is called the child (derived) class, and the class it inherits from is called the parent (base) class. By using inheritance, you can create complex class hierarchies that can help you organize your code and make it more modular and reusable. Overall, inheritance is an essential concept in object-oriented programming, and mastering it can greatly improve your coding skills.

Let's understand inheritance through an example.

Suppose we have a base class called **Animal** that represents a generic animal, with attributes like **name**, **age**, and a method called **speak()**:

```python
class Animal:
    def __init__(self, name, age):
        self.name = name
        self.age = age

    def speak(self):
        print(f"{self.name} makes a noise")
```

Code block: 8.10

Now, we want to create a class **Dog** that represents a dog, which is a specific type of animal. Instead of redefining all the attributes and methods of the **Animal** class, we can inherit them using inheritance:

```python
class Dog(Animal):
    def __init__(self, name, age, breed):
        super().__init__(name, age)
        self.breed = breed

    def speak(self):
        print(f"{self.name} barks")
```

Code block: 8.11

In this example, we define the **Dog** class and inherit from the **Animal** class. We use the **super()** function to call the **__init__** method of the parent class to initialize the **name** and **age** attributes. We also add a new attribute, **breed**, specific to the **Dog** class.

We also override the **speak()** method of the **Animal** class to better fit the behavior of a dog. This is called method overriding and is a common practice when using inheritance.

Now, when we create a **Dog** object, it will have access to both the attributes and methods of the **Animal** class, as well as any new attributes or methods we define in the **Dog** class:

```python
dog1 = Dog("Max", 3, "Labrador")
print(dog1.name)    # Output: Max
print(dog1.age)     # Output: 3
print(dog1.breed)   # Output: Labrador
dog1.speak()        # Output: Max barks
```

Code block: 8.12

Inheritance is a fundamental concept in object-oriented programming that allows for the creation of more specialized classes. It enables code reuse from more general classes while providing the ability to customize or extend their behavior as needed. This makes inheritance a powerful tool for developers to create efficient and effective software solutions.

By using inheritance, developers can create a hierarchy of classes that share common characteristics, allowing for the implementation of complex systems. Additionally, inheritance helps reduce the complexity of code, making it easier to maintain and update over time. Therefore, it is essential to have a solid understanding of inheritance when developing software applications, as it can greatly improve the overall quality of the code and make it more scalable.

Exercise 8.3.1: Simple Inheritance

Implement a class hierarchy for different types of vehicles, using inheritance.

Instructions:

1. Create a base class called **Vehicle** with attributes **make**, **model**, and **year**.
2. Define a method **vehicle_info()** that prints the make, model, and year of the vehicle.
3. Create a class **Car** that inherits from **Vehicle** and has an additional attribute **doors**.
4. Create a class **Motorcycle** that inherits from **Vehicle** and has an additional attribute **type**.
5. Create instances of **Car** and **Motorcycle**, and call the **vehicle_info()** method for each.

Solution:

```python
class Vehicle:
    def __init__(self, make, model, year):
        self.make = make
        self.model = model
        self.year = year

    def vehicle_info(self):
        print(f"{self.year} {self.make} {self.model}")

class Car(Vehicle):
    def __init__(self, make, model, year, doors):
        super().__init__(make, model, year)
        self.doors = doors

class Motorcycle(Vehicle):
    def __init__(self, make, model, year, bike_type):
        super().__init__(make, model, year)
        self.type = bike_type

car1 = Car("Toyota", "Camry", 2020, 4)
car1.vehicle_info()   # Output: 2020 Toyota Camry

motorcycle1 = Motorcycle("Yamaha", "R1", 2019, "Sport")
motorcycle1.vehicle_info()   # Output: 2019 Yamaha R1
```

Code Block: E.8.3.1.1

Exercise 8.3.2: Inheritance and Method Overriding

Create classes representing different types of bank accounts, using inheritance and method overriding.

Instructions:

1. Create a base class **BankAccount** with attributes **balance** and a method **deposit()**.
2. Define a method **withdraw()** that checks if the withdrawal amount is less than or equal to the balance, and updates the balance accordingly.
3. Create a class **SavingsAccount** that inherits from **BankAccount** and has an additional attribute **interest_rate**.
4. Override the **withdraw()** method in **SavingsAccount** to include a withdrawal fee of 1% of the withdrawal amount.
5. Create instances of **BankAccount** and **SavingsAccount**, and test the **deposit()** and **withdraw()** methods.

Solution:

```python
class BankAccount:
    def __init__(self):
        self.balance = 0

    def deposit(self, amount):
        self.balance += amount

    def withdraw(self, amount):
        if amount <= self.balance:
            self.balance -= amount
        else:
            print("Insufficient funds")

class SavingsAccount(BankAccount):
    def __init__(self, interest_rate):
        super().__init__()
        self.interest_rate = interest_rate

    def withdraw(self, amount):
        fee = amount * 0.01
        if amount + fee <= self.balance:
            self.balance -= (amount + fee)
        else:
            print("Insufficient funds")

account1 = BankAccount()
account1.deposit(100)
account1.withdraw(50)
print(account1.balance)   # Output: 50

savings1 = SavingsAccount(0.02)
savings1.deposit(100)
savings1.withdraw(50)
print(savings1.balance)   # Output: 49.5
```

Code Block: E.8.3.2.1

Exercise 8.3.3: Multiple Inheritance

Implement a class hierarchy using multiple inheritance.

Instructions:

1. Create a class **Person** with attributes **first_name** and **last_name**.
2. Create a class **Employee** that inherits from **Person** and has an additional attribute **employee_id**.
3. Create a class **Student** that inherits from **Person** and has an additional attribute **student_id**.
4. Create a class **TeachingAssistant** that inherits from both **Employee** and **Student**.
5. Define a method **get_info()** for each class that returns a string with the person's information.
6. Create an instance of **TeachingAssistant** and call the **get_info()** method.

Solution:

```python
class Person:
    def __init__(self, first_name, last_name):
        self.first_name = first_name
        self.last_name = last_name

    def get_info(self):
        return f"{self.first_name} {self.last_name}"

class Employee(Person):
    def __init__(self, first_name, last_name, employee_id):
        super().__init__(first_name, last_name)
        self.employee_id = employee_id

    def get_info(self):
        return f"{super().get_info()}, Employee ID: {self.employee_id}"

class Student(Person):
    def __init__(self, first_name, last_name, student_id):
        super().__init__(first_name, last_name)
        self.student_id = student_id

    def get_info(self):
        return f"{super().get_info()}, Student ID: {self.student_id}"

class TeachingAssistant(Employee, Student):
    def __init__(self, first_name, last_name, employee_id, student_id):
        Employee.__init__(self, first_name, last_name, employee_id)
        Student.__init__(self, first_name, last_name, student_id)

    def get_info(self):
        return f"{super().get_info()}, Employee ID: {self.employee_id}, Student ID: {self.student_id}"

ta1 = TeachingAssistant("John", "Doe", 1001, 2001)
print(ta1.get_info())  # Output: John Doe, Employee ID: 1001, Student ID: 2001
```

Code Block: E.8.3.3.1

8.4: Polymorphism

Polymorphism is an extremely important concept in object-oriented programming because it allows us to use objects from different classes as if they were objects of the same class, thus making code more flexible and reusable. By treating objects as if they were part of the same class, we can perform the same operations on them, even if they have different internal structures or methods.

In Python, polymorphism can be achieved in a number of ways. One method is through method overloading, which involves defining multiple methods with the same name but different parameters. Another way is through method overriding, where a subclass method replaces a method of the same name in its parent class. Finally, duck typing is a concept in Python where the type of an object is determined by its behavior rather than its class, allowing for greater flexibility in code design.

By using polymorphism in our code, we can create more robust and scalable applications that are able to handle a wide range of input data and perform a variety of operations depending on the objects used. In short, polymorphism is a cornerstone of object-oriented programming and a key tool for software developers to ensure that their code is both flexible and efficient.

8.4.1: Method Overloading:

Method overloading is a programming concept that allows a class to have multiple methods with the same name but different arguments. This feature is not supported in Python in the traditional sense, but there are workarounds that can achieve similar functionality. One such workaround is to provide default values for arguments. This can be helpful when you want to provide a default behavior for a method, but still allow users to override it if they need to.

Another way to achieve similar functionality in Python is by using variable-length argument lists. You can use **args** and ***kwargs** to pass variable-length arguments to a method. This is useful when you are not sure how many arguments a method will need to accept, or when you want to provide a flexible interface for users to interact with your code.

8.4.2: Method Overriding:

Method overriding is a key technique in object-oriented programming that enables a subclass to inherit methods and attributes from its superclass while still allowing it to customize its behavior. This is accomplished by providing a new implementation for a method that has already been defined in the superclass. By doing so, the subclass can extend and modify the functionality of the method to meet its specific needs.

The benefits of method overriding are numerous. First and foremost, it allows for greater flexibility in the design of a program. By being able to customize the behavior of inherited methods, subclasses can tailor their functionality to better fit the specific requirements of their individual use cases. Additionally, method overriding promotes code reuse by enabling subclasses to inherit and modify existing code rather than having to recreate it from scratch.

However, it is important to note that method overriding should be used judiciously. Overriding too many methods can lead to code that is difficult to understand and maintain, and can also lead to unexpected behavior if not done properly. Therefore, it is important to carefully consider the design of a program and the requirements of its use cases before using method overriding.

```python
class Animal:
    def speak(self):
        return "An animal makes a sound"

class Dog(Animal):
    def speak(self):
        return "A dog barks"

animal = Animal()
dog = Dog()

print(animal.speak())   # Output: An animal makes a sound
print(dog.speak())      # Output: A dog barks
```

Code block: 8.13

8.4.3: Duck Typing:

Duck typing is a programming concept that allows you to use an object based on its behavior rather than its class. This means that you can treat any object like a duck, as long as it walks like a duck and quacks like a duck. In other words, if an object behaves like a duck (it has the required methods and properties), you can treat it as a duck, regardless of its actual class.

Python is a language that makes extensive use of duck typing to achieve polymorphism, which allows you to write code that can work with objects of different classes without having to know their exact types in advance. This flexibility is one of the key strengths of Python and has made it a popular choice for developers working on projects with complex, dynamic data structures.

```python
class Circle:
    def __init__(self, radius):
        self.radius = radius

    def area(self):
        return 3.14 * (self.radius ** 2)

class Rectangle:
    def __init__(self, width, height):
        self.width = width
        self.height = height

    def area(self):
        return self.width * self.height

def get_area(shape):
    return shape.area()

circle = Circle(5)
rectangle = Rectangle(4, 6)

print(get_area(circle))     # Output: 78.5
print(get_area(rectangle))  # Output: 24
```

Code block: 8.14

In the example above, the **get_area()** function can calculate the area of any shape object that has an **area()** method, regardless of the shape's class. This demonstrates polymorphism in action through duck typing.

Exercise 8.4.1: Method Overloading

Title: Calculate the area of different shapes

Create a class **Shape** that has a method **area()** which accepts different numbers of arguments to calculate the area of different shapes (circle and rectangle).

Instructions:

1. Create a class **Shape**.
2. Implement an **area()** method that accepts different numbers of arguments.
3. If there's one argument, treat it as the radius of a circle and calculate the area of the circle.
4. If there are two arguments, treat them as the width and height of a rectangle and calculate the area of the rectangle.
5. If no arguments or more than two arguments are provided, raise a **ValueError** with an appropriate error message.

```python
class Shape:
    def area(self, *args):
        if len(args) == 1:
            radius = args[0]
            return 3.14 * (radius ** 2)
        elif len(args) == 2:
            width, height = args
            return width * height
        else:
            raise ValueError("Invalid number of arguments")

shape = Shape()
print(shape.area(5))         # Output: 78.5
print(shape.area(4, 6))      # Output: 24
try:
    print(shape.area())
except ValueError as e:
    print(e)                 # Output: Invalid number of arguments
```

Code block: E.8.4.1.1

Exercise 8.4.2: Method Overriding

Title: Custom **__str__** method for **Person** and **Employee**

Create a class **Person** and a subclass **Employee**. Both classes should have a custom **__str__** method to return a string representation of the object.

Instructions:

1. Create a class **Person** with attributes **first_name** and **last_name**.
2. Implement a custom **__str__** method for the **Person** class that returns the full name.
3. Create a subclass **Employee** that inherits from **Person** and has an additional attribute **position**.
4. Implement a custom **__str__** method for the **Employee** class that returns the full name and position.

Solution:

```python
class Person:
    def __init__(self, first_name, last_name):
        self.first_name = first_name
        self.last_name = last_name

    def __str__(self):
        return f"{self.first_name} {self.last_name}"

class Employee(Person):
    def __init__(self, first_name, last_name, position):
        super().__init__(first_name, last_name)
        self.position = position

    def __str__(self):
        return f"{super().__str__()}, Position: {self.position}"

person = Person("John", "Doe")
employee = Employee("Jane", "Doe", "Software Engineer")

print(person)     # Output: John Doe
print(employee)   # Output: Jane Doe, Position: Software Engineer
```

Code block: E.8.4.2.1

Exercise 8.4.3: Duck Typing

Title: Implement a **SoundMaker** function

Description**:** Create a **SoundMaker** function that accepts an object and calls its **make_sound()** method, demonstrating duck typing.

Instructions**:**

1. Create a class **Dog** with a method **make_sound()** that returns the string "Woof!".
2. Create a class **Cat** with a method **make_sound()** that returns the string "Meow!".
3. Implement a function **SoundMaker()** that accepts an object and calls its **make_sound()** method.
4. Test the **SoundMaker()** function with instances of both **Dog** and **Cat**.

Solution:

```python
class Dog:
    def make_sound(self):
        return "Woof!"

class Cat:
    def make_sound(self):
        return "Meow!"

def SoundMaker(animal):
    return animal.make_sound()

dog = Dog()
cat = Cat()

print(SoundMaker(dog))   # Output: Woof!
print(SoundMaker(cat))   # Output: Meow!
```

Code block: E.8.4.3.1

In this exercise, we have created two classes, **Dog** and **Cat**, each with their own **make_sound()** method. The **SoundMaker()** function takes an object as an argument and calls its **make_sound()** method without needing to know the exact type of the object. This demonstrates the concept of duck typing in Python.

8.5: Encapsulation

Encapsulation is one of the most fundamental principles of object-oriented programming. It is the process of combining data (attributes) and methods that operate on that data within a single unit, usually a class, to create a cohesive and well-organized system.

By using encapsulation, we can limit access to certain parts of the object, which can help prevent unwanted interference or modification of the object's internal state. This can be especially useful in large and complex systems, where keeping track of the state of different objects can become difficult. Additionally, encapsulation can make it easier to modify and update the code, as changes to one part of the code will have less of an impact on the rest of the system. Overall, encapsulation is a powerful technique that can help create more robust and maintainable code.

Encapsulation is achieved by using private and protected access specifiers for attributes and methods. In Python, there is no strict concept of private or protected members, but we follow certain conventions to indicate the intended access level:

8.5.1: Public members:

By default, all members of a class are public, meaning they can be accessed from anywhere inside and outside the class. However, it is important to note that making all members public can lead to potential security issues, as sensitive information may be accessed or modified by unauthorized users. To mitigate this risk, it is recommended to use access modifiers such as private or protected for sensitive members, and only provide public access to necessary members. Additionally, using encapsulation techniques such as getters and setters can help ensure that data is accessed and modified in a controlled and secure manner.

8.5.2: Protected members:

If a member is intended to be accessed only from within the class and its subclasses, its name should be prefixed with a single underscore (_). This is known as a convention and it is widely used in Python. However, it is important to note that this convention does not actually prevent access to the member from outside the class or its subclasses. In such cases, it is recommended to use name mangling, a technique that adds a prefix to the name of the member to make it harder to access from outside the class. Name mangling is achieved by prefixing the member name with two underscores (__) and a suffix of one or more underscores. For example, a member named "my_var" would become "_MyClass__my_var" in the class called "MyClass". Note that this technique should be used with caution, as it can make the code harder to read and maintain.

8.5.3: Private members:

If a member is intended to be accessed only within the class (not even by subclasses), its name should be prefixed with double underscores (__). Python does provide a limited form of privacy by name mangling, which makes it difficult but not impossible to access the member from outside the class.

It is important to understand that name mangling is not a form of security. It is simply a convention used to discourage accidental access to private members. In fact, name mangling can be easily circumvented by accessing the member using its mangled name.

In addition, Python also allows for protected members, which can be accessed by subclasses but not from outside the class. These members are prefixed with a single underscore (_).

It is worth noting that the use of private and protected members is not necessary in all cases. In many cases, it is perfectly acceptable to make all members public. However, in larger projects or projects with multiple developers, the use of private and protected members can help to prevent unintended modifications to critical parts of the code.

Example:

```python
class BankAccount:
    def __init__(self, account_number, balance):
        self._account_number = account_number
        self.__balance = balance

    def deposit(self, amount):
        self.__balance += amount

    def withdraw(self, amount):
        if amount <= self.__balance:
            self.__balance -= amount
        else:
            print("Insufficient funds")

    def get_balance(self):
        return self.__balance

account = BankAccount("12345", 1000)
account.deposit(500)
account.withdraw(300)

print(account.get_balance())  # Output: 1200
```

Code block: 8.15

In this example, the **BankAccount** class has an attribute **__balance**, which is intended to be private. We have provided methods like **deposit()**, **withdraw()**, and **get_balance()** to manipulate the balance, thus preventing direct access to the attribute. Note that **_account_number** is a protected member, which is not enforced by Python but signifies that it should be treated as protected by convention.

Exercise 8.5.1: Create a Simple Employee Class

In this exercise, you'll create a simple Employee class that uses encapsulation to protect its data members.

Instructions:

1. Create a class called **Employee**.
2. Define the following private attributes: **__first_name**, **__last_name**, and **__salary**.
3. Create a constructor that takes **first_name**, **last_name**, and **salary** as parameters and initializes the private attributes.
4. Create public methods **get_first_name()**, **get_last_name()**, and **get_salary()** that return the respective attributes.
5. Create a method **get_full_name()** that returns the employee's full name, which is the combination of the first and last name.

Solution:

```python
class Employee:
    def __init__(self, first_name, last_name, salary):
        self.__first_name = first_name
        self.__last_name = last_name
        self.__salary = salary

    def get_first_name(self):
        return self.__first_name

    def get_last_name(self):
        return self.__last_name

    def get_salary(self):
        return self.__salary

    def get_full_name(self):
        return self.__first_name + " " + self.__last_name

employee = Employee("John", "Doe", 50000)
print(employee.get_full_name())   # Output: John Doe
```

Code block: E.8.5.1.1

Exercise 8.5.2: Implementing a Circle Class

In this exercise, you'll create a **Circle** class that uses encapsulation to protect its data members and provide methods to manipulate them.

Instructions:

1. Create a class called **Circle**.
2. Define the following private attributes: **__radius** and **__pi** (use the value 3.14159 for pi).
3. Create a constructor that takes **radius** as a parameter and initializes the private attribute **__radius**.
4. Create public methods **get_radius()** and **get_pi()** that return the respective attributes.
5. Create methods **calculate_area()** and **calculate_circumference()** that return the area and circumference of the circle, respectively.

Solution:

```python
class Circle:
    def __init__(self, radius):
        self.__radius = radius
        self.__pi = 3.14159

    def get_radius(self):
        return self.__radius

    def get_pi(self):
        return self.__pi

    def calculate_area(self):
        return self.__pi * self.__radius ** 2

    def calculate_circumference(self):
        return 2 * self.__pi * self.__radius

circle = Circle(5)
print(circle.calculate_area())           # Output: 78.53975
print(circle.calculate_circumference())  # Output: 31.4159
```

Code block: E.8.5.2.1

Exercise 8.5.3: Creating a Password Protected Account

In this exercise, you'll create an **Account** class that uses encapsulation to protect its data members and requires a password to access certain methods.

Instructions:

1. Create a class called **Account**.
2. Define the following private attributes: **__account_number**, **__balance**, and **__password**.
3. Create a constructor that takes **account_number**, **balance**, and **password** as parameters and initializes the private attributes.
4. Create public methods **get_account_number()** and **get_balance()** that return the respective attributes.
5. Create a method **validate_password(self, password)** that returns **True** if the given password matches the account's password, and **False** otherwise.
6. Create a method **withdraw(self, amount, password)** that checks if the password is correct using **validate_password()**, and if so, subtracts the given amount from the balance.

Solution:

```python
class Account:
    def __init__(self, account_number, balance, password):
        self.__account_number = account_number
        self.__balance = balance
        self.__password = password

    def get_account_number(self):
        return self.__account_number

    def get_balance(self):
        return self.__balance

    def validate_password(self, password):
        return self.__password == password

    def withdraw(self, amount, password):
        if self.validate_password(password):
            self.__balance -= amount
            return True
        return False

account = Account("123456", 1000, "secret123")
print(account.get_account_number())   # Output: 123456
print(account.get_balance())          # Output: 1000

if account.withdraw(200, "secret123"):
    print("Withdrawal successful!")
    print("New balance:", account.get_balance())  # Output: 800
else:
    print("Incorrect password or insufficient funds.")
```

Code block: E.8.5.3.1

In this exercise, you've created an **Account** class that demonstrates the concept of encapsulation by protecting its data members and requiring a password for certain operations.

As we conclude Chapter 8, it's important to recognize the significance of Object-Oriented Programming (OOP) in Python. Through OOP, we can create more organized, maintainable, and scalable code. In this chapter, we have explored the key OOP concepts:

1. **Classes and Objects**: The fundamentals of creating custom data types and instances in Python.
2. **Attributes and Methods**: How to store data and define behaviors within classes.
3. **Inheritance**: A way to create new classes from existing ones, promoting code reusability.
4. **Polymorphism**: Leveraging the power of inheritance and method overriding to create flexible code that can handle different types of objects.
5. **Encapsulation**: Protecting the internal state and implementation of a class, providing a well-defined interface for interacting with it.

By applying these principles in your Python programs, you can create code that is easier to understand, debug, and extend. Don't forget to practice implementing these concepts through exercises and real-world projects to gain a deeper understanding of OOP in Python.

As you move forward, remember that Python is a versatile language that supports multiple programming paradigms. Combining OOP with other approaches, such as functional programming, can help you further refine and tailor your code to suit various situations and requirements. See you in the next chapter. Happy coding!

CHAPTER 9: Error Handling and Exceptions

When working with Python, it is important to note that you will inevitably encounter errors or exceptions. These errors are a crucial aspect of programming, as they aid in identifying issues within your code and provide opportunities to learn how to fix them. By learning how to handle exceptions, you will become more proficient at troubleshooting and debugging your code.

Moreover, the ability to create custom exceptions will allow for more efficient and effective error management throughout your program. In this chapter, we will delve into the different types of errors you may encounter, the various methods of handling exceptions, and how custom exceptions can improve your overall programming experience.

9.1 Common Python Errors

Before diving into error handling, let's first understand the most common types of errors you might encounter when writing Python code. Errors can be broadly categorized into two types: Syntax Errors and Exceptions.

When we talk about syntax errors, we are referring to errors that occur when our code violates the rules of Python syntax. These errors are usually easy to spot, as they will often be accompanied by an error message that points directly to the problematic line of code. On the other hand, exceptions are errors that occur when our code is syntactically correct, but something goes wrong during execution.

These types of errors can be much more difficult to track down, as they can be caused by a wide range of factors, including incorrect input values or unexpected changes to the state of the program. While it can be frustrating to encounter errors in your Python code, understanding the different types of errors and how to handle them is an essential part of becoming a proficient Python developer.

9.1.1: Syntax Errors:

Syntax errors, also known as parsing errors, occur when the Python interpreter fails to understand your code due to incorrect syntax. These errors usually arise from typing mistakes, incorrect indentation, or misuse of language constructs. Some examples of syntax errors are:

- Missing colons in control structures like **if**, **for**, and **def**.
- Mismatched parentheses, brackets, or quotes.
- Incorrect indentation, which is particularly important in Python.

Example of a syntax error:

```
if x > 0
    print("x is positive")
```

Code block: 9.1

In this example, there's a missing colon at the end of the **if** statement, which leads to a syntax error.

9.1.2: Exceptions:

Exceptions are runtime errors that occur when your code encounters an unexpected situation or condition. Unlike syntax errors, exceptions do not necessarily result from incorrect code syntax. Instead, they may arise from unanticipated circumstances during code execution, such as file I/O errors, invalid user input, or unhandled edge cases. Some common exceptions include:

- **TypeError**: Raised when you perform an operation on an inappropriate data type.
- **NameError**: Raised when you try to use a variable or function that has not been defined.
- **ValueError**: Raised when you pass an invalid argument to a function.
- **ZeroDivisionError**: Raised when you attempt to divide a number by zero.
- **FileNotFoundError**: Raised when you try to open a file that does not exist.

Example of an exception:

```
x = 0
y = 10
result = y / x
```

Code block: 9.2

In this example, we're trying to divide **y** by **x**. Since **x** is zero, a **ZeroDivisionError** exception will be raised.

By understanding these common errors, you'll not only be better equipped to diagnose and fix issues in your Python programs, but you'll also be able to write more efficient and effective code. In the following sections, we'll learn how to handle exceptions and even create our own custom exceptions to improve error handling in our code.

By doing so, we'll not only improve the stability and reliability of our programs, but we'll also be able to write more robust and scalable applications that can handle a wide range of inputs and use cases. This can be particularly important when working with large datasets or complex algorithms, where even a small error can have a significant impact on the final output. As such, mastering error handling in Python is an essential skill for any programmer or data scientist looking to take their skills to the next level.

Exercise 9.1.1: Identify Syntax Errors

In this exercise, you will be given a Python code snippet containing syntax errors. Your task is to identify and fix these errors.

Instructions:

1. Read the following code snippet.
2. Identify the syntax errors present in the code.
3. Fix the syntax errors and run the corrected code to make sure it works as intended.

Code Snippet:

```
x = 5
y = 10

if x < y
    print("x is less than y")
```

Code block: E.9.1.1.1

Solution:

```
x = 5
y = 10

if x < y:
    print("x is less than y")
```

Code block: E.9.1.1.2

Output:

x is less than y

```
x is less than y
```

Code block: E.9.1.1.3

Exercise 9.1.2: Identify Exception Errors

In this exercise, you will be given a Python code snippet containing an exception error. Your task is to identify the exception and fix the code to prevent the error.

Instructions:

1. Read the following code snippet.
2. Identify the exception error in the code.
3. Fix the exception error and run the corrected code to make sure it works as intended.

Code Snippet:

```python
numerator = 7
denominator = 0

result = numerator / denominator
print(result)
```

Code block: E.9.1.2.1

Solution:

```python
numerator = 7
denominator = 0

if denominator != 0:
    result = numerator / denominator
    print(result)
else:
    print("Cannot divide by zero")
```

Code block: E.9.1.2.2

Output:

```
Cannot divide by zero
```

Code block: E.9.1.2.3

Exercise 9.1.3: Raise Custom Exception

In this exercise, you will create a function that raises a custom exception when an invalid input is detected.

Instructions:

1. Create a function called **validate_age** that takes one argument, **age**.
2. Inside the function, check if **age** is less than 0.
3. If **age** is less than 0, raise a **ValueError** exception with the message "Age cannot be negative."
4. Call the function with a positive and a negative age value to test the exception handling.

Code Snippet:

```
def validate_age(age):
    # Your code here

validate_age(25)
validate_age(-5)
```

Code block: E.9.1.3.1

Solution:

```python
def validate_age(age):
    if age < 0:
        raise ValueError("Age cannot be negative.")

try:
    validate_age(25)
    validate_age(-5)
except ValueError as ve:
    print(ve)
```

Code block: E.9.1.3.2

Output:

```
Age cannot be negative.
```

Code block: E.9.1.3.3

9.2: Handling Exceptions with try and except

Python is an incredibly versatile programming language that offers a wide range of tools and features to developers. One such feature is the ability to handle exceptions using the **try** and **except** statements. These statements allow developers to monitor code execution and provide a means of dealing with exceptions that may arise during runtime.

When a block of code is enclosed within a **try** statement, Python executes the code, monitoring it for any exceptions that might occur. This means that even if an exception is raised, the program can continue to execute without crashing or causing other issues. Instead, the program execution jumps to the appropriate **except** block, which is designed to handle the specific exception or tuple of exceptions that was raised.

It is important to note that the **try** statement should be followed by one or more **except** blocks. These blocks are designed to handle the specific exceptions that may arise during runtime. Additionally, you can also use an optional **else** block to specify code that will be executed if no exceptions occur. This is useful for cases where you want to perform additional actions if the code runs without issue.

Finally, there is the **finally** block. This block is used to specify code that will be executed regardless of whether an exception occurred or not. This is useful for cases where you need to clean up resources or perform other actions that are required regardless of the outcome of the program execution.

In sumary, the **try** and **except** statements are valuable tools for any Python developer. By using these statements, you can handle exceptions in a way that allows your program to continue executing even if errors occur. Additionally, the **else** and **finally** blocks provide additional functionality that can be used to make your code more robust and reliable.

Here's the general syntax for a **try-except** statement:

```
try:
    # code that might raise an exception
except ExceptionType1:
    # code to handle exception of type ExceptionType1
except (ExceptionType2, ExceptionType3):
    # code to handle exception of type ExceptionType2 or ExceptionType3
else:
    # code to be executed if no exception was raised
finally:
    # code that will always be executed, regardless of exceptions
```

Code block: 9.3

An example of using the **try** and **except** statements to handle exceptions:

```python
try:
    numerator = 10
    denominator = 0
    result = numerator / denominator
except ZeroDivisionError:
    print("Cannot divide by zero")
except Exception as e:
    print("An unknown error occurred:", e)
else:
    print("The division was successful:", result)
finally:
    print("Thank you for using our division calculator")
```

Code block: 9.4

In this example, we first try to perform the division operation. If a **ZeroDivisionError** occurs, we print an informative message. If any other exception occurs, we catch it using the **Exception** class, which is a base class for all built-in exceptions, and print an unknown error message. If no exception occurs, we print the result of the division. Finally, we print a message thanking the user for using our division calculator, regardless of whether an exception occurred or not.

When using **try** and **except**, it's important to handle the exceptions that you expect to occur and allow the others to be propagated up the call stack. This is because catching too many exceptions or defining a broad exception class like **Exception** can lead to difficulty identifying and resolving issues in the code. Moreover, it can even hide legitimate errors that should be addressed.

For instance, when catching a broad exception class like **Exception**, it's possible that we may miss a specific exception that was not anticipated or that we don't know how to handle. In such a case, the exception will be caught and processed by the general exception handler, which may not be able to handle the specific exception adequately. As a result, the error may be hidden or even worse, the code may continue to run with an unexpected behavior.

On the other hand, when we catch only the exceptions that we expect to occur, we can handle them specifically and provide better error messages to the users. This can help to improve the quality of the code and make it easier to maintain and debug. Additionally, it can make the code more robust against unexpected changes in the environment or input data.

Therefore, it's recommended to be cautious when defining exception handlers and only catch the exceptions that we can handle appropriately. This can help to make the code more reliable and easier to maintain in the long run.

Exercise 9.2.1: Safe File Reading

Write a program that tries to read a file given by the user and prints the contents of the file. If the file is not found or cannot be read, display an error message.

Instructions:

1. Prompt the user for a filename.
2. Use a try-except block to open the file and read its content.
3. If a FileNotFoundError occurs, print an error message.
4. Otherwise, print the contents of the file.
5. Close the file.

Solution:

```python
filename = input("Enter the filename: ")

try:
    with open(filename, "r") as file:
        content = file.read()
except FileNotFoundError:
    print(f"Error: The file '{filename}' does not exist or could not be found.")
else:
    print("File contents:")
    print(content)
```

Code block: E.9.2.1.1

Output:

```
Enter the filename: sample.txt
File contents:
This is a sample text file.
```

Code block: E.9.2.1.2

Exercise 9.2.2: Safe Division

Write a program that takes two numbers as input and performs division. If a division by zero occurs, display an error message.

Instructions:

1. Prompt the user for two numbers.
2. Use a try-except block to perform the division.
3. If a ZeroDivisionError occurs, print an error message.
4. Otherwise, print the result of the division.

Solution:

```python
numerator = float(input("Enter the numerator: "))
denominator = float(input("Enter the denominator: "))

try:
    result = numerator / denominator
except ZeroDivisionError:
    print("Error: Division by zero is not allowed.")
else:
    print(f"The result is {result}.")
```

Code block: E.9.2.2.1

Output:

```
Enter the numerator: 10
Enter the denominator: 0
Error: Division by zero is not allowed.
```

Code block: E.9.2.2.2

Exercise 9.2.3: Safe List Indexing

Write a program that tries to access an element in a list by its index given by the user. If an IndexError occurs, display an error message.

Instructions:

1. Create a list with some elements.
2. Prompt the user for an index.
3. Use a try-except block to access the element at the given index.
4. If an IndexError occurs, print an error message.
5. Otherwise, print the accessed element.

Solution:

```python
my_list = [10, 20, 30, 40, 50]
index = int(input("Enter the index of the element to retrieve: "))

try:
    element = my_list[index]
except IndexError:
    print(f"Error: The index '{index}' is out of range.")
else:
    print(f"The element at index {index} is {element}.")
```

Code block: E.9.2.3.1

Output:

```
Enter the index of the element to retrieve: 7
Error: The index '7' is out of range.
```

Code block: E.9.2.3.2

9.3: Raising Exceptions

In Python, exceptions are events that can occur when there is an error or an exceptional condition during the execution of a program. These can be caused by a variety of factors, such as incorrect input or an unexpected event. As we have seen before, Python automatically raises exceptions when it encounters an error. However, you can also manually raise exceptions in your code by using the **raise** statement. This is particularly useful when you want to enforce certain conditions or constraints in your program, such as checking for valid input or ensuring that certain resources are available before executing a piece of code.

To raise an exception, you can use the **raise** keyword followed by the exception class or an instance of the exception class you want to raise. This can be helpful in providing additional context for the error, such as specifying the type of error that occurred or providing a custom message to the user. By raising exceptions in your code, you can improve its robustness and make it more reliable, ensuring that it can handle a wide range of inputs and conditions.

Here is the basic syntax for raising an exception:

```
raise ExceptionClass("Error message")
```

Code block: 9.5

For example, you can raise a **ValueError** exception if you want to enforce that a certain value should be within a specific range:

```
def validate_age(age):
    if age < 0 or age > 150:
        raise ValueError("Invalid age: Age must be between 0 and 150")

try:
    validate_age(-5)
except ValueError as ve:
    print(ve)
```

Code block: 9.6

In this example, the **validate_age** function checks if the given age is within the valid range (0 to 150). If it is not, a **ValueError** exception is raised with a custom error message. We then use a try-except block to call the function and handle the exception if it occurs.

When you raise an exception in your code, you are essentially signaling that something has gone wrong and the normal flow of your program cannot continue. This means that the control is transferred to the nearest enclosing try-except block, which is a block of code designed to handle exceptions in a specific way. If there is no such block, the program will terminate, and the error message will be displayed.

But why is it so important to raise exceptions in the first place? Well, doing so can actually help you create more robust and error-resilient code. By detecting and handling errors early on in the code, you can prevent them from causing unexpected behavior or even crashing your program altogether. This can save you time and frustration in the long run, as well as make your code more reliable and easier to maintain.

Exercise 9.3.1: Raising Exceptions for Invalid Input

Title: Validate User Input

Description: Write a function called **validate_input** that takes a string as its input and raises a **ValueError** exception if the input string contains any special characters (e.g., !, @, #, etc.).

Instructions:

1. Create a function **validate_input** that takes a string **input_str**.
2. Check if the input string contains any special characters.
3. If it does, raise a **ValueError** with a custom error message.
4. Test the function with valid and invalid inputs using a try-except block.

Solution:

```python
import string

def validate_input(input_str):
    if any(char in string.punctuation for char in input_str):
        raise ValueError("Invalid input: The input should not contain special ch
aracters")

try:
    validate_input("HelloWorld!")
except ValueError as ve:
    print(ve)

try:
    validate_input("HelloWorld")
except ValueError as ve:
    print(ve)
```

Code block: E.9.3.1.1

Output:

```
Invalid input: The input should not contain special characters
```

Code block: E.9.3.1.2

Exercise 9.3.2: Raising Exceptions for Invalid Passwords

Title: Password Strength Checker

Description: Create a function called **validate_password** that checks if a given password is strong. A strong password is defined as having at least 8 characters, containing at least one uppercase letter, one lowercase letter, one digit, and one special character. Raise a **ValueError** exception if the password does not meet these criteria.

Instructions:

1. Create a function **validate_password** that takes a string **password**.
2. Check if the password meets the criteria for a strong password.
3. If it does not, raise a **ValueError** with a custom error message.
4. Test the function with valid and invalid passwords using a try-except block.

Solution:

```python
import string

def validate_password(password):
    if len(password) < 8:
        raise ValueError("Invalid password: Password must have at least 8 characters")

    if not any(char.isupper() for char in password):
        raise ValueError("Invalid password: Password must have at least one uppercase letter")

    if not any(char.islower() for char in password):
        raise ValueError("Invalid password: Password must have at least one lowercase letter")

    if not any(char.isdigit() for char in password):
        raise ValueError("Invalid password: Password must have at least one digit")

    if not any(char in string.punctuation for char in password):
        raise ValueError("Invalid password: Password must have at least one special character")

try:
    validate_password("WeakPwd1")
except ValueError as ve:
    print(ve)

try:
    validate_password("StrongPwd1!")
except ValueError as ve:
    print(ve)
```

Code block. E.9.3.2.1

Output:

```
Invalid password: Password must have at least one special character
```

Code block: E.9.3.2.2

Exercise 9.3.3: Raising Exceptions for Invalid Email Addresses

Title: Email Validator

Description: Create a function called **validate_email** that checks if a given email address is valid. A valid email address should have the following format: **<username>@<domain>.<tld>**. Raise a **ValueError** exception if the email address does not meet these criteria.

Instructions:

1. Create a function **validate_email** that takes a string **email**.
2. Check if the email address is valid.
3. If it is not, raise a **ValueError** with a custom error message.
4. Test the function with valid and invalid email addresses using a try-except block.

Solution:

```python
import re

def validate_email(email):
    email_regex = r'^[a-zA-Z0-9._%+-]+@[a-zA-Z0-9.-]+\.[a-zA-Z]{2,}$'
    if not re.match(email_regex, email):
        raise ValueError("Invalid email address")

try:
    validate_email("invalid_email.com")
except ValueError as ve:
    print(ve)

try:
    validate_email("valid.email@example.com")
except ValueError as ve:
    print(ve)
```

Code block: E.9.3.3.1

Output:

```
Invalid email address
```

Code block: E.9.3.3.2

9.4: Custom Exceptions

Python is a programming language that allows for the creation of custom exceptions. By doing this, developers can tailor their exceptions to specific error conditions. Custom exceptions can provide more detailed error messages that are easier for programmers to understand and handle. This is important because it allows for quicker identification and resolution of errors in code.

To create a custom exception in Python, you will need to define a new class that inherits from the base **Exception** class or one of its subclasses. This new class should include any additional attributes or methods that are needed to properly describe the exception. By doing this, you can ensure that the custom exception provides all the necessary information to help identify and solve any issues that may arise during development.

In addition, custom exceptions can be used to differentiate between different types of errors that may occur in your code. For example, you can create a custom exception for errors related to file input/output, and another custom exception for errors related to network connectivity. This makes it easier to handle different types of errors in specific ways, which can lead to more efficient and effective error handling overall.

Overall, the ability to create custom exceptions is an important feature of Python that can greatly improve the development process. By providing more descriptive error messages and allowing for more targeted error handling, custom exceptions can help to streamline the debugging process and ensure that code runs smoothly and efficiently.

Here's an example of how to create a simple custom exception:

```python
class CustomError(Exception):
    pass
```

Code block: 9.7

In this example, we define a new class named **CustomError** that inherits from the **Exception** class. The **pass** statement indicates that the class is empty and doesn't provide any additional functionality.

Now, let's say you want to add a custom error message to your exception:

```python
class CustomError(Exception):
    def __init__(self, message):
        self.message = message
        super().__init__(message)
```

Code block: 9.8

In this case, we've overridden the **__init__** method of the **Exception** class, allowing us to provide a custom error message when the exception is raised. The **super().__init__(message)** line calls the **__init__** method of the parent **Exception** class, passing the custom error message to it.

You can raise your custom exception just like any other exception:

```python
raise CustomError("This is a custom error message.")
```

Code block: 9.9

When creating custom exceptions, it is a good practice to use descriptive names that indicate the nature of the error, and to provide helpful error messages to make debugging easier.

Example:

Let's say you're creating a program that deals with user accounts, and you want to define a custom exception for when a user tries to create an account with an invalid email address. You could create a custom exception like this:

```python
class InvalidEmailError(Exception):
    def __init__(self, email):
        self.email = email
        message = f"The email address '{email}' is invalid."
        super().__init__(message)

# Usage
try:
    raise InvalidEmailError("invalid_email.com")
except InvalidEmailError as e:
    print(e)
```

Code block: 9.10

In this example, we've created a custom exception named **InvalidEmailError**. When raising this exception, we pass the invalid email address as an argument, which is then used to create a custom error message.

Exercise 9.4.1: Create a custom exception for negative numbers

Title: NegativeNumberError

Description: Create a custom exception called **NegativeNumberError** that takes a number as an argument and returns an error message indicating that the number is negative.

Instructions:

1. Define a custom exception called **NegativeNumberError**.
2. Raise the **NegativeNumberError** exception if a given number is negative.
3. Catch and handle the exception by printing the error message.

Solution:

```python
class NegativeNumberError(Exception):
    def __init__(self, number):
        self.number = number
        message = f"The number {number} is negative."
        super().__init__(message)

def check_positive_number(number):
    if number < 0:
        raise NegativeNumberError(number)
    else:
        print(f"The number {number} is positive.")

try:
    check_positive_number(-5)
except NegativeNumberError as e:
    print(e)
```

Code block: E.9.4.1.1

Output:

```
The number -5 is negative.
```

Code block: E.9.4.1.2

Exercise 9.4.2: Create a custom exception for empty input strings

Title: EmptyStringError

Description: Create a custom exception called **EmptyStringError** that takes a string as an argument and returns an error message indicating that the input string is empty.

Instructions:

1. Define a custom exception called **EmptyStringError**.
2. Raise the **EmptyStringError** exception if a given string is empty.
3. Catch and handle the exception by printing the error message.

Solution:

```python
class EmptyStringError(Exception):
    def __init__(self):
        message = "The input string is empty."
        super().__init__(message)

def check_non_empty_string(input_string):
    if not input_string:
        raise EmptyStringError()
    else:
        print(f"The input string is not empty.")

try:
    check_non_empty_string("")
except EmptyStringError as e:
    print(e)
```

Code block: E.9.4.2.1

Output:

```
The input string is empty.
```

Code block: E.9.4.2.2

Exercise 9.4.3: Create a custom exception for invalid usernames

Title: InvalidUsernameError

Description: Create a custom exception called **InvalidUsernameError** that takes a username as an argument and returns an error message indicating that the username is invalid.

Instructions:

1. Define a custom exception called **InvalidUsernameError**.
2. Create a function that validates a given username.
3. Raise the **InvalidUsernameError** exception if the username is invalid.
4. Catch and handle the exception by printing the error message.

Solution:

```python
class InvalidUsernameError(Exception):
    def __init__(self, username):
        self.username = username
        message = f"The username '{username}' is invalid."
        super().__init__(message)

def validate_username(username):
    if len(username) < 5:
        raise InvalidUsernameError(username)
    else:
        print(f"The username '{username}' is valid.")

try:
    validate_username("usr")
except InvalidUsernameError as e:
    print(e)
```

Code block: E.9.4.3.1

Output:

```
The username 'usr' is invalid.
```

Code block: E 9.4.3.2

As we conclude Chapter 9, let's recap the main concepts we covered:

1. Common Python Errors: We've looked at different types of errors, such as syntax errors, type errors, and name errors. Understanding these errors is essential to debug code effectively.
2. Handling Exceptions with try and except: We've learned how to use the **try** and **except** blocks to handle exceptions gracefully. This technique allows your program to continue executing even when encountering an error.
3. Raising Exceptions: We discussed how to raise exceptions using the **raise** statement, which is useful when you need to indicate that an error has occurred in your code.
4. Custom Exceptions: Finally, we covered how to create custom exception classes to handle specific situations in your code more effectively. Custom exceptions allow you to provide more descriptive error messages and handle errors in a more targeted way.

By understanding and implementing these concepts, you will be able to write more robust and maintainable Python code. Error handling is a crucial aspect of programming, as it helps you anticipate and deal with unexpected situations that may arise during the execution of your programs. Keep practicing and applying these concepts in your projects to become more proficient in handling errors and exceptions in Python.

See you in next chapter: "Python Best Practices."

CHAPTER 10: Python Best Practices

As we approach the end of this book, it is important to note that the best practices for Python programmers are critical to the success of any project. While there are many best practices that programmers can follow, the ones presented here are essential to maintaining efficient, readable, and maintainable code. In this chapter, we will delve deeper into PEP 8, the official style guide for Python code, and explore how it can be used to improve your code.

Furthermore, we will discuss other critical topics such as code organization, documentation, and testing. It is essential to understand these concepts in their entirety, as they will be crucial in ensuring that your Python projects are a success.

10.1 PEP 8 - Style Guide for Python Code

PEP 8 is the Python Enhancement Proposal that provides a set of guidelines and conventions for writing Python code. The primary purpose of PEP 8 is to make the code more readable and maintainable by providing a consistent style. Although PEP 8 is not a strict requirement, it is highly recommended to follow these guidelines to ensure that your code is easily understood by others, and even by yourself, in the future.

Some of the key aspects of PEP 8 include:

10.1.1: Indentation:

When writing code, it is important to maintain consistent formatting. This can be achieved by using 4 spaces per indentation level, rather than mixing spaces and tabs. By doing so, the code becomes more readable and easier to understand for others who may need to work with the code in the future. Additionally, consistent formatting can help prevent errors and make debugging easier. Therefore, it is highly recommended to use 4 spaces per indentation level for all code you write.

Example:

```
# Good
def my_function(arg1, arg2):
    result = arg1 + arg2
    return result

# Bad
def my_function(arg1, arg2):
   result = arg1 + arg2
   return result
```

Code block: 10.1

10.1.2: Maximum Line Length:

One way to improve code readability is to limit the number of characters per line. This can be achieved by setting a maximum line length of 79 characters. By doing this, the code becomes easier to read, especially when working with multiple files side by side. It allows for a more organized and structured codebase, as developers can quickly scan through the code and identify potential issues or areas for improvement.

Additionally, keeping the code within a certain length limit can also help with debugging and testing, as it minimizes the need for horizontal scrolling and makes it easier to spot errors.

Example:

```
# Good
def my_function(long_arg1, long_arg2,
                long_arg3, long_arg4):
    result = (
        long_arg1 + long_arg2
        - long_arg3 * long_arg4
    )
    return result

# Bad
def my_function(long_arg1, long_arg2, long_arg3, long_arg4): result = long_arg1 + long_arg2 - long_arg3 * long_arg4; return result
```

Code block: 10.2

10.1.3: Imports:

When writing code, it is important to organize your imports in a clear and consistent manner. By placing your imports at the top of the file, you can make it easier for other developers to understand what external dependencies your code relies on. However, it's not enough to simply list your imports in a random order. To maximize readability, imports should be separated by a blank line, and organized in a specific order.

First, you should list any standard library imports that your code requires. These are built-in modules that come with the Python language, such as "os" or "sys".

Next, you should list any third-party imports that your code requires. These are external modules that you have installed using a package manager like "pip". Examples of third-party modules might include "numpy" or "pandas".

Finally, you should list any local application or library-specific imports that your code requires. These are modules that you have written yourself, or that are specific to your particular project.

By following this organization scheme, you can help ensure that your code is easy to read and understand, even for developers who are unfamiliar with your project. So don't forget to take a little extra time to organize your imports properly!

Example

```
# Good
import os
import sys

import requests

from my_module import my_function

# Bad
import os, sys
from my_module import my_function
import requests
```

Code block: 10.3

10.1.4: Whitespace:

When writing code, it is important to use whitespace effectively. This means that while you should avoid using excessive whitespace, you should also use it to separate logical sections of your code. For example, you can use a single blank line to separate functions, methods, or class definitions. By using whitespace in this way, you can make your code more organized and easier to read.

In addition to separating code sections, it is also important to use whitespace around operators and after commas in lists, tuples, or dictionaries. This makes the code more readable and easier to understand, especially if someone else needs to review or modify it in the future.

Example

```
# Good
my_list = [1, 2, 3, 4]
result = x * y + z

# Bad
my_list=[1,2,3,4]
result=x*y+z
```

Code block. 10.4

10.1.5: Naming Conventions:

- Variables and function names should be lowercase, with words separated by underscores (e.g., **my_variable**, **my_function**).
- Constants should be in uppercase, with words separated by underscores (e.g., **MY_CONSTANT**).
- Class names should use the CapWords (PascalCase) convention (e.g., **MyClass**).
- Method names should be lowercase, with words separated by underscores (e.g., **my_method**).

Example

```
# Good
class MyClass:
    my_variable = 10

    def my_method(self):
        pass

# Bad
class myclass:
    MyVariable = 10

    def MyMethod(self):
        pass
```

Code block 10.5

10.1.6: Comments:

When writing code, it is important to use comments to explain the purpose of the code, especially when it might be difficult to understand. Comments help other programmers who may need to work with your code to understand how it works and what it does.

It is recommended to use inline comments sparingly, as adding too many comments can make the code harder to read. When adding inline comments, it is important to separate them from the code with at least two spaces.

Always start comments with a capital letter and end with a period. This helps to maintain consistency and readability within your code, and can make it easier for others to understand what you are trying to accomplish.

In summary, comments are a vital part of writing good code, and can help to make your code more understandable and maintainable. So don't forget to add comments to your code!

Example

```
# Good
def my_function():
    # Calculate the result based on some logic.
    result = 42
    return result

# Bad
def my_function():
    result = 42   # Calculate the result based on some logic.
    return result
```

Code block 10.6

10.1.7: Docstrings:

Using docstrings, or triple-quoted strings, is a great way to provide documentation for your modules, classes, functions, and methods. This can help others understand the purpose and usage of your code more effectively, which can be especially important when working on projects with others or contributing to open-source projects.

Not only can good documentation make it easier for others to use and build on your code, but it can also make it easier for you to come back to your own code later on and remember how it works. In fact, many developers consider good documentation to be just as important as good code itself, since it can help ensure that your code is maintainable and usable in the long run. So, if you're not already using docstrings in your code, it might be worth taking the time to start incorporating them into your programming practices.

Example

```python
# Good
def my_function(arg1, arg2):
    """
    Calculate the sum of two arguments.

    Args:
        arg1 (int): The first argument.
        arg2 (int): The second argument.

    Returns:
        int: The sum of the two arguments.
    """
    return arg1 + arg2

# Bad
def my_function(arg1, arg2):
    # Calculate the sum of two arguments
    return arg1 + arg2
```

Code block: 10.7

These are just a few of the many guidelines provided by PEP 8. It is recommended to read the full PEP 8 document (https://www.python.org/dev/peps/pep-0008/) to familiarize yourself with all the guidelines and apply them consistently in your Python projects.

Exercise 10.1.1: PEP 8 Indentation

In this exercise, you'll practice fixing the indentation in a Python script to follow the PEP 8 guidelines.

Instructions: Fix the indentation in the given Python script. The script should have 4 spaces for each indentation level.

Solution:

```python
def my_function(arg1, arg2):
    result = arg1 + arg2
    return result

if __name__ == "__main__":
    num1 = 5
    num2 = 10
    sum_result = my_function(num1, num2)
    print(f"The sum of {num1} and {num2} is {sum_result}.")
```

Code block: E.10.1.1.1

Output:

```
The sum of 5 and 10 is 15.
```

Code block: E.10.1.1.2

Exercise 10.1.2: PEP 8 Imports

In this exercise, you'll practice organizing imports according to PEP 8 guidelines.

Instructions: Reorganize the given imports in the Python script so that they follow the PEP 8 guidelines.

Solution:

```
import os
import sys

import requests

from my_module import my_function

print("Imports organized according to PEP 8.")
```

Code block: E.10.1.2.1

Output:

```
Imports organized according to PEP 8.
```

Code block: E.10.1.2.2

Note: The output will differ based on your system and the actual "my_module" you import.

Exercise 10.1.3: PEP 8 Naming Conventions

In this exercise, you'll practice applying PEP 8 naming conventions to a Python script.

Instructions: Update the given Python script so that it follows the PEP 8 naming conventions for variables, functions, and classes.

Solution:

```python
class MyClass:
    my_variable = 10

    def my_method(self):
        return self.my_variable * 2

def main():
    my_instance = MyClass()
    result = my_instance.my_method()
    print(f"The result is: {result}")

if __name__ == "__main__":
    main()
```

Code block: E 10.1.3.1

Output:

```
The result is: 20
```

Code block: E 10.1.3.2

10.2: Code Commenting and Documentation

As a Python developer, it is essential to write clean, maintainable, and well-documented code. By doing so, you can help ensure that your code can be easily understood by other developers, regardless of their level of expertise. Providing detailed documentation and commenting your code can be particularly helpful in this regard, as it can help to break down complex concepts into more digestible pieces.

One of the key benefits of commenting your code is that it can make it easier to debug and maintain. By providing clear and concise comments alongside your code, you can help other developers to quickly understand your thought process and identify any issues that may be present. This can also be helpful in situations where you may be working on a project with other developers, as it can help to ensure that everyone is on the same page.

In addition to commenting your code, it's also important to provide detailed documentation. This can include information on how to use the code, what it does, and any potential issues that may arise. By providing detailed documentation, you can help to ensure that your code is usable by other developers, regardless of their level of experience.

Overall, the importance of code commenting and documentation cannot be overstated. By taking the time to write clean, maintainable, and well-documented code, you can help to ensure that your code is easily understood, debugged, and maintained, both now and in the future.

10.2.1: Inline comments:

Inline comments are used to explain a single line of code or a specific operation within a line. These comments should be brief, clear, and start with a '#' symbol, followed by a single space. You should place the inline comment on the same line as the code it's describing or on the line immediately above it.

Example:

```
x = 5  # Assigning the value 5 to variable x
```

Code block: 10.8

10.2.2: Block comments:

Block comments are used to provide a detailed explanation of a block of code or a specific algorithm. These comments should be placed above the code block they describe and should be indented to the same level as the code. Each line of a block comment should start with a '#' symbol and a single space.

Example:

```
# Here, we are initializing the variables and
# calculating the sum of two numbers.
x = 5
y = 10
sum_result = x + y
```

Code block: 10.9

10.2.3: Docstrings:

Docstrings, or documentation strings, are used to provide documentation for modules, classes, functions, and methods. They are placed immediately after the definition of the module, class, function, or method they describe. Docstrings are enclosed in triple quotes (either single or double) and can span multiple lines.

Example:

```
def add_numbers(x, y):
    """
    This function takes two numbers as arguments,
    calculates their sum, and returns the result.

    Args:
        x (int): The first number
        y (int): The second number

    Returns:
        int: The sum of x and y
    """
    return x + y
```

Code block: 10.10

In summary, code commenting and documentation are essential practices for writing maintainable and easy-to-understand code. By following these guidelines, you can ensure that your code is well-organized and accessible to others, making it easier to collaborate and maintain your projects.

To expand on this, code commenting involves adding comments to your code to explain its purpose, functionality, and any other important details. This can help other developers who may need to work with your code in the future to understand what your code does and how it works. Additionally, by commenting your code, you can make it easier for yourself to understand your own code when you come back to it after a long time.

Documentation, on the other hand, involves creating a separate document that explains how to use your code, what it does, and any other important details. This can be especially helpful for larger projects where there are many different components and features. By creating good documentation, you can make it easier for other developers to understand how your code fits together and how to use it effectively.

In conclusion, code commenting and documentation are key practices for creating maintainable and understandable code. By investing time and effort into these practices, you can make it easier for yourself and others to work with your code and ensure that your projects are successful in the long term.

Exercise 10.2.1: Inline Commenting

Title: Inline Commenting Practice

Improve the readability of the provided code by adding inline comments to describe the operations.

Instructions:

1. Read the given code.
2. Identify key operations in the code.
3. Add inline comments to describe the operations.

Solution:

```python
# Import the math module
import math

radius = 5  # Set the radius of the circle

# Calculate the area of the circle
area = math.pi * (radius ** 2)

# Calculate the circumference of the circle
circumference = 2 * math.pi * radius

# Print the area and circumference
print("Area:", area)
print("Circumference:", circumference)
```

Code block: E.10.2.1.1

Output:

```
Area: 78.53981633974483
Circumference: 31.41592653589793
```

Code block: E.10.2.1.2

Exercise 10.2.2: Block Commenting

Title: Block Commenting Practice

Enhance the given code by adding block comments to explain the different sections of the code.

Instructions:

1. Read the given code.
2. Identify distinct sections in the code.

3. Add block comments to describe the sections.

Solution:

```python
# Initialize variables
num1 = 10
num2 = 20
num3 = 30

# Perform arithmetic operations
sum_result = num1 + num2 + num3
product = num1 * num2 * num3
average = sum_result / 3

# Print the results
print("Sum:", sum_result)
print("Product:", product)
print("Average:", average)
```

Code block: E.10.2.2.1

Output:

```
Sum: 60
Product: 6000
Average: 20.0
```

Code block: E.10.2.2.2

Exercise 10.2.3: Writing Docstrings

Title: Writing Docstrings Practice

Write a function with a descriptive docstring.

Instructions:

1. Create a function called **multiply_numbers** that takes two numbers as arguments and returns their product.
2. Write a clear and descriptive docstring for the function.

Solution:

```python
def multiply_numbers(x, y):
    """
    This function takes two numbers as arguments,
    calculates their product, and returns the result.

    Args:
        x (int): The first number
        y (int): The second number

    Returns:
        int: The product of x and y
    """
    return x * y

# Test the function
result = multiply_numbers(5, 10)
print("Product:", result)
```

Code block: E.10.2.3.1

Output:

```
Product: 50
```

Code block: E.10.2.3.2

10.3: Naming Conventions

In Python, it is incredibly important to use clear and descriptive names for variables, functions, classes, and modules. Doing so will make your code more readable and maintainable, which is crucial for any project. However, it's not just about using descriptive names - it's also about being consistent throughout your code. By adopting a consistent naming convention, you can help other developers understand and contribute to your project more efficiently. Luckily, As we described before, Python has a set of widely-accepted naming conventions, which are covered in PEP 8. This section will provide a more detailed discussion of these conventions, and how they can be applied to your code to make it more readable and maintainable.

10.3.1: Variables and functions:

Use lowercase letters and separate words with underscores (snake_case). This convention makes your code easy to read and understand. For example:

```python
filename = "example.txt"
counter = 0

def process_data(data):
    pass
```

Code block: 10.11

10.3.2: Constants:

Constants should be named using uppercase letters and underscores to separate words. This convention makes it easy to distinguish constants from other variables.

```python
PI = 3.14159
MAX_SIZE = 1000
```

Code block: 10.12

10.3.3: Classes:

Use CamelCase (capitalizing the first letter of each word) for class names. This convention helps distinguish class names from variable and function names.

```
class MyClass:
    pass

class CustomerData:
    pass
```

Code block 10.13

10.3.4: Modules:

Module names should be lowercase and can use underscores if it improves readability. This convention keeps module names consistent with variable and function names.

```
# my_module.py
import my_module
```

Code block 10.14

10.3.5: Private variables and methods:

To indicate that a variable or method is private (i.e., not meant to be accessed directly), you can use a single leading underscore. This is a convention rather than a strict rule, but it helps communicate the intended use of the variable or method to other developers.

```
class MyClass:
    def __init__(self):
        self._private_variable = 42

    def _private_method(self):
        pass
```

Code block: 10.15

By following these naming conventions, you'll improve the readability and maintainability of your Python code. This can save time and effort in the long run, especially when working in a team or revisiting code after a period of time. It's important to be consistent with these conventions throughout your codebase to ensure a coherent and professional appearance.

This consistency can also aid in debugging and troubleshooting, as well as reduce the likelihood of errors or confusion caused by inconsistent naming. Additionally, adhering to standard naming conventions can make it easier for others to understand and contribute to your code, as they will be familiar with the naming conventions used. Therefore, it's recommended to take the time to learn and follow these conventions, as they can have a significant impact on the quality and usability of your code.

Exercise 10.3.1: Identifying Incorrect Naming Conventions

In this exercise, you will analyze a given code snippet and identify the incorrect naming conventions. Then, you'll correct the code to follow proper naming conventions.

Instructions:

1. Identify the incorrect naming conventions in the given code snippet.
2. Correct the code to follow proper naming conventions.

```
class car:
    def __init__(self, make, Model, year):
        self.Make = make
        self.model = Model
        self.Year = year

    def get_car_info(self):
        return f"{self.Year} {self.Make} {self.model}"
```

Code block: E.10.3.1.1

Solution:

```
class Car:
    def __init__(self, make, model, year):
        self.make = make
        self.model = model
        self.year = year

    def get_car_info(self):
        return f"{self.year} {self.make} {self.model}"
```

Code block: E.10.3.1.2

Exercise 10.3.2: Applying Naming Conventions

In this exercise, you will write a simple Python script that calculates the area of a circle using the proper naming conventions.

Instructions:

1. Define a constant **PI** with a value of 3.14159.
2. Create a function **calculate_area(radius)** that takes the radius as an argument and returns the area of a circle.
3. Call the function with the radius of 5 and print the result.

Solution:

```
PI = 3.14159

def calculate_area(radius):
    return PI * radius ** 2

radius = 5
area = calculate_area(radius)
print(f"The area of the circle with radius {radius} is {area:.2f}")
```

Code block: E.10.3.2.1

Output:

```
The area of the circle with radius 5 is 78.54
```

Code block: E.10.3.2.2

Exercise 10.3.3: Refactoring Code with Proper Naming Conventions

In this exercise, you will refactor a provided code snippet by applying proper naming conventions.

Instructions:

1. Refactor the given code snippet by applying proper naming conventions.
2. Ensure that the code works correctly after refactoring.

```
class student:
    def __init__(s, name, age):
        s.Name = name
        s.age = age

    def display_info(s):
        print(f"Name: {s.Name}, Age: {s.age}")

stud = student("John", 20)
stud.display_info()
```

Code block: E.10.3.3.1

Solution:

```
class Student:
    def __init__(self, name, age):
        self.name = name
        self.age = age

    def display_info(self):
        print(f"Name: {self.name}, Age: {self.age}")

student_instance = Student("John", 20)
student_instance.display_info()
```

Code block: E.10.3.3.2

Output:

```
Name: John, Age: 20
```

Code block: E.10.3.3.3

10.4: Code Reusability and Modularization

In this section, we will discuss the importance of code reusability and modularization, which are crucial to writing clean, maintainable, and efficient Python programs.

10.4.1: Code Reusability:

Code reusability refers to writing code in a way that can be used multiple times without having to rewrite it. Reusable code is efficient, less prone to errors, and easier to maintain. By creating functions, classes, and modules that perform specific tasks, you can reuse the code throughout your project, as well as in future projects.

Benefits of code reusability:

1. Reduces code duplication: When you write reusable code, you reduce the amount of duplicated code in your project, which in turn makes your codebase easier to maintain.
2. Improves readability: Reusable code is usually well-organized and easy to understand, which makes it easier for other developers to read and understand your code.
3. Simplifies code maintenance: When you need to make changes to a piece of reusable code, you only need to modify it in one place, which reduces the risk of introducing new bugs.
4. Enhances productivity: Writing reusable code speeds up the development process, as you spend less time writing code from scratch.

10.4.2: Modularization:

Modularization is the process of dividing your code into smaller, independent units called modules. Each module performs a specific task and can be developed, tested, and maintained independently of the others. In Python, a module is simply a file containing Python code.

Benefits of modularization:

1. Easier code organization: Modularization helps you organize your code into logical units, making it easier to understand and manage.
2. Improved collaboration: When working on a team, modularization allows multiple developers to work on different parts of the codebase simultaneously without conflicts.
3. Enhanced maintainability: Modular code is easier to maintain and update, as you can modify individual modules without affecting the entire codebase.

4. Simplified testing and debugging: With modularization, you can test and debug individual modules separately, which speeds up the development process and reduces the likelihood of introducing new bugs.

10.4.3: Best Practices:

To achieve code reusability and modularization in Python, follow these best practices:

1. Write reusable functions and classes: Create functions and classes that perform specific tasks and can be reused throughout your project.
2. Use Python modules and packages: Organize your code into modules and packages to make it easy to import and reuse functionality across different parts of your project.
3. Leverage existing libraries: Whenever possible, use existing Python libraries and modules to avoid reinventing the wheel.
4. Adhere to Python best practices: Follow the PEP 8 style guide, use appropriate naming conventions, and document your code to ensure it is easily understandable and maintainable.

By focusing on code reusability and modularization, you will write cleaner, more efficient, and maintainable Python code, making your projects more enjoyable and successful.

10.4.4: Code Reusability Examples:

Let's look at some examples to illustrate code reusability and modularization in Python.

Example 1: Reusable function

Let's create a reusable function to calculate the factorial of a given number.

```python
def factorial(n):
    if n == 0:
        return 1
    else:
        return n * factorial(n - 1)

print(factorial(5))   # Output: 120
print(factorial(7))   # Output: 5040
```

Code block: 10.16

The **factorial** function can be used multiple times without rewriting the code, making it reusable.

Example 2: Modularization using modules

Suppose we have two Python files: **math_operations.py** and **main.py**.

In **math_operations.py**, we define some functions for common mathematical operations:

```python
# math_operations.py

def add(a, b):
    return a + b

def subtract(a, b):
    return a - b

def multiply(a, b):
    return a * b

def divide(a, b):
    return a / b
```

Code block: 10.17

In **main.py**, we can import the **math_operations** module and use its functions:

```python
# main.py

import math_operations

print(math_operations.add(2, 3))        # Output: 5
print(math_operations.subtract(7, 2))   # Output: 5
print(math_operations.multiply(3, 4))   # Output: 12
print(math_operations.divide(8, 2))     # Output: 4.0
```

Code block: 10.18

By organizing our code into separate modules, we make it more modular and easier to maintain.

Example 3: Modularization using packages

We can also organize our code using packages. Suppose we have the following directory structure:

```
my_package/
    __init__.py
    math_operations.py
main.py
```

Code block: 10.19

In **math_operations.py**, we have the same functions as before. In **main.py**, we can import the **my_package.math_operations** module and use its functions:

```python
# main.py

import my_package.math_operations

print(my_package.math_operations.add(2, 3))        # Output: 5
print(my_package.math_operations.subtract(7, 2))   # Output: 5
print(my_package.math_operations.multiply(3, 4))   # Output: 12
print(my_package.math_operations.divide(8, 2))     # Output: 4.0
```

Code block: 10.20

Using packages, which are a collection of related modules or classes, can further help us organize our code. By dividing our code into smaller, more manageable pieces, we can make it more modular and easier to maintain. Additionally, packages provide a way to group related functionality together, which can make it easier for other developers to understand and use our code.

Furthermore, packages can also allow for better code reuse and can help prevent naming conflicts with other code. Thus, using packages is a useful technique for improving the organization, maintainability, and usability of our codebase.

Exercise 10.4.1: Reusable function for Fibonacci series

Create a reusable function that calculates the first n numbers of the Fibonacci series.

Instructions:

1. Define a function called **fibonacci_series** that takes a single argument, n.
2. Calculate the first n numbers of the Fibonacci series using a loop.
3. Print the series.

Solution:

```python
def fibonacci_series(n):
    series = []
    a, b = 0, 1
    for _ in range(n):
        series.append(a)
        a, b = b, a + b
    return series

print(fibonacci_series(7))
```

Code block: E.10.4.1.1

Output:

```
[0, 1, 1, 2, 3, 5, 8]
```

Code block: E.10.4.1.2

Exercise 10.4.2: Create a reusable module for string manipulation

Create a Python module named **string_manipulation.py** containing reusable functions for various string operations.

Instructions:

1. In **string_manipulation.py**, define the following functions:
   - **reverse_string**: Takes a string and returns the reverse of the string.
   - **uppercase_string**: Takes a string and returns the string with all letters in uppercase.
   - **lowercase_string**: Takes a string and returns the string with all letters in lowercase.
2. In another Python file, import the **string_manipulation** module.
3. Use the functions to manipulate a given string and print the results.

Solution:

```python
# string_manipulation.py

def reverse_string(s):
    return s[::-1]

def uppercase_string(s):
    return s.upper()

def lowercase_string(s):
    return s.lower()
```

Code block: E.10.4.2.1

```python
# main.py

import string_manipulation

text = "Python is Awesome"

print(string_manipulation.reverse_string(text))
print(string_manipulation.uppercase_string(text))
print(string_manipulation.lowercase_string(text))
```

Code block: E.10.4.2.2

Output:

```
emosewA si nohtyP
PYTHON IS AWESOME
python is awesome
```

Code block: E.10.4.2.3

Exercise 10.4.3: Organize a package for geometry calculations

Create a package named **geometry** containing Python modules for calculating areas of different shapes.

Instructions:

Create a directory named **geometry** with the following structure:

```
geometry/
    __init__.py
    circles.py
    rectangles.py
```

Code block: E.10.4.3.1

In **circles.py**, define a function named **area_circle** that takes the radius as an argument and returns the area of the circle.

In **rectangles.py**, define a function named **area_rectangle** that takes width and height as arguments and returns the area of the rectangle.

In another Python file, import the **geometry** package and use the functions to calculate the areas of a circle and a rectangle.

Solution:

```python
# geometry/circles.py

import math

def area_circle(radius):
    return math.pi * radius * radius
```

Code block: E.10.4.3.2

```python
# geometry/rectangles.py

def area_rectangle(width, height):
    return width * height
```

Code block: E.10.4.3.3

```python
# main.py

from geometry.circles import area_circle
from geometry.rectangles import area_rectangle

print(area_circle(5))
print(area_rectangle(4, 6))
```

Code block: E.10.4.3.4

Output:

```
78.53981633974483
24
```

Code block: E.10.4.3.5

In conclusion, this chapter aimed to introduce you to Python best practices that will help you write cleaner, more maintainable, and more efficient code. We started with PEP 8, the Style Guide for Python Code, which provides guidelines on how to format your code to make it more readable and consistent with the Python community standards.

We also discussed the importance of code commenting and documentation. Properly documenting your code makes it easier for others (and your future self) to understand your code and its purpose. We covered various types of comments, such as inline comments, block comments, and docstrings.

Next, we explored naming conventions in Python, which play a crucial role in making your code more understandable and maintainable. We learned about the conventions for variables, constants, functions, classes, modules, and packages.

Lastly, we delved into code reusability and modularization. Writing modular, reusable code is essential for creating more efficient and maintainable programs. We looked at how to create reusable functions, modules, and packages that can be easily imported and used in other projects.

By adhering to these best practices, you will become a more proficient Python programmer and contribute to creating high-quality, maintainable code. As you continue to develop your skills, always be open to learning and improving, and never hesitate to ask for help or feedback from the Python community.

CHAPTER 11: Project: Build a Simple Application

In this chapter, we will put into practice the concepts and techniques you've learned throughout this book by building a simple application. This project will help you solidify your understanding of Python fundamentals and give you a taste of real-world programming.

To start off, we will discuss the importance of proper planning when it comes to programming. We'll go over the various steps involved in the planning process and how to organize your thoughts effectively. We'll also touch on the importance of having a clear and concise project scope to ensure that you stay on track throughout the development process.

Once we have a clear plan in place, we'll move on to the implementation phase. This is where you'll get hands-on experience with writing code in Python. We'll start with the basics, such as data types and control structures, and gradually move on to more complex topics like object-oriented programming and database integration.

Finally, we'll test the application to ensure that it performs as expected. We'll cover various testing methodologies, including unit testing and integration testing, and show you how to use them effectively. By the end of this chapter, you'll have a solid understanding of Python programming and be ready to tackle more complex projects in the future.

11.1: Planning Your Project

Before diving into the code, it's essential to plan your project thoroughly. A well-planned project will save you time and effort in the long run, as it helps you foresee potential problems, create a roadmap, and organize your thoughts. Here are some steps you should follow during the planning phase:

1. Define the scope of the project: Begin by outlining the project's main objective and what you want your application to accomplish. Clearly defining the project's scope will help you stay focused and avoid feature creep.
2. Identify the key functionalities: Break down the project into smaller tasks and functionalities. This will make it easier to manage and track your progress. Create a list of the core features that your application must have and any additional features that can be added later if time permits.
3. Design the user interface (UI): Sketch the user interface of your application, whether it's a command-line interface (CLI) or a graphical user interface (GUI). Think about how users will interact with your application and what kind of input you'll need from them. Consider user experience (UX) principles to ensure your application is user-friendly.
4. Choose the appropriate data structures: Based on your project's requirements, decide which data structures will be the most suitable for storing and managing your data. This could include lists, dictionaries, tuples, or custom classes and objects.
5. Plan the architecture: Organize your project's structure by deciding how to break down your code into modules, classes, and functions. This will help you create a modular and reusable codebase that is easier to maintain and extend.
6. Plan the testing strategy: Determine how you'll test your application to ensure it's working correctly and meeting the project requirements. Plan to write unit tests for individual functions and integration tests for the entire application.

Once you've completed the planning phase, you'll have a solid foundation for your project and can proceed with confidence. In the next topics, we'll discuss the actual implementation of the application, starting with setting up the project environment.

11.1.1: TaskMaster Application

In this chapter, we'll guide you through building a simple command-line application called "TaskMaster" that allows users to manage their to-do list. This application will help you apply the concepts and techniques learned throughout the book.

The TaskMaster application will have the following features:

1. Add a new task to the list.
2. View the list of tasks.
3. Mark a task as completed.
4. Remove a task from the list.
5. Save the list of tasks to a file.

Now, let's revisit the planning steps with this project in mind:

1. **Define the scope of the project:** The TaskMaster application will allow users to manage a to-do list through a command-line interface.
2. **Identify the key functionalities:**
    - Add a new task.
    - View the list of tasks.
    - Mark a task as completed.
    - Remove a task from the list.
    - Save the list of tasks to a file.
3. **Design the user interface (UI):** The application will have a command-line interface (CLI) with text-based menus and prompts for user input.
4. **Choose the appropriate data structures:** We'll use a list of dictionaries to store tasks, where each dictionary represents a task with keys for the task description and its completion status.
5. **Plan the architecture:** We'll create a main module (**taskmaster.py**) that contains the application's core logic and a helper module (**file_handler.py**) to handle saving and loading tasks from a file.
6. **Plan the testing strategy:** We'll write unit tests for individual functions and integration tests for the entire application to ensure it's working correctly and meeting the project requirements.

With the planning phase completed, we can proceed to the implementation phase. In the next topics, we'll start building the TaskMaster application step by step, beginning with setting up the project environment and creating the basic structure of the application.

11.2: Implementing the TaskMaster Project

Now that we have planned our TaskMaster project, we can start implementing it. In this topic, we'll set up the project environment, create the basic structure of the application, and implement the main functionalities.

1. Set up the project environment: Create a new directory for the project and navigate to it in your command-line interface. Then, create a virtual environment and activate it. This step is essential for managing dependencies and ensuring that your project runs smoothly.
2. Create the basic structure: We'll need two Python modules for this project: **taskmaster.py** and **file_handler.py**. Create these two files in the project directory.
3. Implement the **taskmaster.py** module: This module will contain the core logic of the application. Start by importing the necessary modules and defining the main menu function, which will display the available options to the user.

```
import file_handler

def main_menu():
    print("Welcome to TaskMaster!")
    print("Please choose an option:")
    print("1. Add a new task")
    print("2. View tasks")
    print("3. Mark a task as completed")
    print("4. Remove a task")
    print("5. Save tasks to file")
    print("6. Exit")

if __name__ == "__main__":
    main_menu()
```

Code block: 11.1

Implement the **file_handler.py** module: This module will handle saving and loading tasks from a file. Start by defining two functions: **save_tasks_to_file()** and **load_tasks_from_file()**.

```
def save_tasks_to_file(tasks, filename="tasks.txt"):
    # Save tasks to file

def load_tasks_from_file(filename="tasks.txt"):
    # Load tasks from file and return them
```

Code block: 11.2

Implement the TaskMaster functionalities: Now, add the necessary functions for adding, viewing, marking as completed, and removing tasks. Also, implement the logic for saving tasks to a file and loading them when the application starts.

Add error handling: Implement error handling for invalid user input, file I/O issues, and any other potential exceptions.

Test the application: Thoroughly test the application to ensure it works correctly and meets the project requirements. Be sure to fix any issues that you encounter during the testing phase.

Refactor and optimize the code: Review your code, refactor it if necessary, and optimize it for better readability, maintainability, and performance.

With these steps completed, you should have a fully functioning TaskMaster application that allows users to manage their to-do list through a command-line interface. In the next topic, we'll discuss how to package and distribute the application.

11.3: Testing and Debugging the TaskMaster Project

In this topic, we will discuss the importance of testing and debugging the TaskMaster project to ensure that it works as expected and is free of bugs. We'll go through some basic testing strategies and debugging techniques to help you identify and fix any issues in your code.

11.3.1: Unit testing:

Unit testing involves testing individual functions or components of your application in isolation to ensure they work as intended. For TaskMaster, you can create a separate file called **test_taskmaster.py** and write unit tests for each function in your **taskmaster.py** and **file_handler.py** modules. You can use Python's built-in **unittest** module to create and run your tests.

Example:

Create a file **test_taskmaster.py** with the following content:

```python
import unittest
from taskmaster import TaskMaster
from file_handler import FileHandler

class TestTaskMaster(unittest.TestCase):

    def test_create_task(self):
        taskmaster = TaskMaster()
        taskmaster.create_task('Buy milk')
        self.assertEqual(taskmaster.tasks[0]['task'], 'Buy milk')

    def test_save_tasks(self):
        taskmaster = TaskMaster()
        taskmaster.create_task('Buy milk')
        taskmaster.create_task('Walk the dog')
        FileHandler.save_tasks(taskmaster.tasks)
        saved_tasks = FileHandler.load_tasks()
        self.assertEqual(saved_tasks, taskmaster.tasks)

if __name__ == '__main__':
    unittest.main()
```

Code block: 11.3

11.3.2: Integration testing:

Integration testing focuses on testing the interaction between different components of your application to ensure they work correctly together. For TaskMaster, this means testing the interaction between the main menu, task handling functions, and file I/O functions. You can write integration tests in your **test_taskmaster.py** file as well.

Example:

You can add an integration test to the **test_taskmaster.py** file:

```
def test_add_and_complete_task(self):
    taskmaster = TaskMaster()
    taskmaster.create_task('Buy milk')
    taskmaster.mark_task_complete(0)
    self.assertTrue(taskmaster.tasks[0]['completed'])
```

Code block: 11.4

11.3.3: Manual testing:

While automated tests are essential, manual testing is also important to ensure that your application works as expected in real-world usage scenarios. To perform manual testing, run your TaskMaster application and interact with it as a user would. Try different combinations of inputs, edge cases, and unexpected scenarios to identify any issues that your automated tests may have missed.

Example:

For manual testing, you'll run the TaskMaster application and interact with it, simulating various user inputs and scenarios. For example:

- Adding tasks
- Completing tasks
- Saving tasks to a file
- Loading tasks from a file

11.3.4: Debugging:

If you encounter any issues or bugs during testing, use Python's built-in debugger, **pdb**, to help identify the cause of the problem. You can insert breakpoints in your code using the **pdb.set_trace()** function, which allows you to pause the execution of your program at a specific point and examine the state of your variables, step through your code line by line, and evaluate expressions. This can help you track down the source of the issue and fix it.

Example:

Suppose you have an issue in the **taskmaster.py** file, and you want to debug it. Add a breakpoint using **pdb.set_trace()**:

```python
import pdb

def mark_task_complete(self, task_id):
    for task in self.tasks:
        if task['id'] == task_id:
            task['completed'] = True
            print(f"Task {task['task']} marked as complete.")
            break
    else:
        print("Task not found.")
        pdb.set_trace()  # Add the breakpoint here
```

Code block: 11.5

11.3.5: Refactoring:

After identifying and fixing any issues in your code, review it to see if there are any opportunities for refactoring or optimization. This might include simplifying complex code, improving the readability of your code, or making your code more efficient.

Example:

Refactor the task creation code to make it more readable:

```
pythonCopy code# Original code
task = {'id': self.task_counter, 'task': task_description, 'completed': False}

# Refactored code
task = {
    'id': self.task_counter,
    'task': task_description,
    'completed': False
}
```

Code block: 11.6

11.3.6: Re-testing:

After making any changes to your code, be sure to re-run your automated tests and perform additional manual testing to ensure that your changes didn't introduce any new issues or regressions.

Example:

After refactoring, run your tests again to ensure that everything still works as expected:

```
python test_taskmaster.py
```

Code block: 11.7

This should display the test results, showing whether your tests passed or failed. If any tests fail, you should debug and fix the issues before proceeding.

By following these testing and debugging strategies, you'll ensure that your TaskMaster application is reliable, robust, and free of any critical issues. In the next topic, we'll discuss how to package and distribute your application.

11.4: Deployment and Distribution:

In this topic, we will discuss how to deploy and distribute the TaskMaster application to users.

For a small-scale Python application like TaskMaster, there are a few ways to package and distribute it to users:

1. Distribute the source code
2. Create a Python package
3. Package the application as an executable

11.4.1: Distribute the source code:

This is the simplest method. You can zip the source code files and share the zip file with the users. They will need to have Python installed on their systems to run the application. To run the TaskMaster application, users will need to execute the following command:

```
python main.py
```

Code block: 11.8

11.4.2: Create a Python package:

Another option is to create a Python package for the TaskMaster application. This way, users can install the package using **pip** and run the application from the command line. To create a package, follow these steps:

a. Install **setuptools** and **wheel**:

```
pip install setuptools wheel
```

Code block: 11.9

b. Create a **setup.py** file in the project directory with the following content:

```python
from setuptools import setup, find_packages

setup(
    name="taskmaster",
    version="0.1.0",
    packages=find_packages(),
    entry_points={
        "console_scripts": [
            "taskmaster = main:main",
        ],
    },
)
```

Code block: 11.10

c. Build the package:

```
python setup.py sdist bdist_wheel
```

Code block: 11.11

This will create a **dist** directory containing the distribution files.

d. Users can then install the package using **pip**:

```
pip install /path/to/dist/taskmaster-0.1.0-py3-none-any.whl
```

Code block: 11.12

Once installed, users can run the TaskMaster application by typing **taskmaster** in the command line.

11.4.3: Package the application as an executable:

You can package the TaskMaster application as a standalone executable using tools like PyInstaller or cx_Freeze. This way, users won't need to have Python installed on their systems.

For example, using PyInstaller:

a. Install PyInstaller:

```
pip install pyinstaller
```

Code block: 11.13

b. Package the application:

```
pyinstaller --onefile main.py
```

Code block: 11.14

This will create a standalone executable file **main.exe** (or **main** on Unix-based systems) in the **dist** directory.

c. Distribute the executable to users, who can run the TaskMaster application by double-clicking the file or executing it from the command line.

In summary, you can deploy and distribute the TaskMaster application using various methods, depending on the needs of your users and your project requirements.

11.5: Chapter 11 Conclusion

In conclusion, Chapter 11 provided a detailed and comprehensive guide on how to build a simple yet functional Python application called TaskMaster. The guide began by emphasizing the importance of planning and breaking down the project into smaller, manageable tasks. These tasks were then implemented step-by-step, ensuring that the core functionality of the application was built before moving on to designing a simple user interface.

Throughout the guide, we highlighted the significance of testing and debugging to ensure the application's reliability and correctness. By following these procedures, you can ensure that your Python application meets its goals and functions as intended.

Furthermore, the guide also discussed various deployment and distribution methods for the TaskMaster application. These methods included distributing the source code, creating a Python package, and packaging the application as an executable. Each of these methods was thoroughly analyzed, and their pros and cons were discussed to help you make an informed decision on which method is best suited for your project.

In addition, the guide also emphasized the importance of applying the principles and guidelines discussed throughout the book to create robust, user-friendly applications that meet your goals. It is essential to keep in mind the importance of planning, implementation, testing, and deployment to ensure the success of your future Python projects.

By following the best practices and knowledge you've gained throughout the book, you can create Python applications that are not only functional and reliable but also user-friendly and efficient. With this guide, you now have the tools and knowledge to embark on your own Python projects with confidence and success.

CHAPTER 12: Next Steps in Your Python Journey

Congratulations on completing this book, which has given you a solid foundation in Python programming. Having said that, the world of Python is vast and there are still many topics that you can delve into to advance your understanding and expertise. In this chapter, we will briefly touch upon some advanced Python topics and resources that can aid you in your quest to become a Python expert. We hope that this chapter will serve as an overview of these topics and provide you with a stepping stone for further exploration and continued learning.

One advanced topic that is worth exploring is object-oriented programming (OOP). OOP is a programming paradigm that focuses on the creation of objects that encapsulate data and functionality. It is a powerful technique that can help you create more modular and reusable code. Another area of interest is data visualization. Python has many libraries that can help you create stunning visualizations of your data, such as Matplotlib, Seaborn, and Plotly.

In addition to these topics, there are also many resources available to help you continue your Python journey. Online communities like Reddit and Stack Overflow can be great places to ask questions and learn from others. There are also many blogs, podcasts, and YouTube channels dedicated to Python that can provide you with valuable insights and perspectives. Finally, attending conferences and meetups can be a great way to network with other Python developers and learn about the latest trends and developments in the field.

We hope that this chapter has given you a taste of the many exciting possibilities that await you in the world of Python. Remember, learning is a lifelong journey, and there is always more to discover and explore. Keep coding and have fun!

In this chapter, we will briefly discuss some advanced Python topics and resources that can help you on your journey to becoming a Python expert. This chapter aims to provide an overview of these topics and serve as a stepping stone for your continued learning.

12.1: Advanced Python Topics

1. **Advanced data structures**: While we have covered lists, dictionaries, sets, and tuples, there are more specialized data structures available in Python, such as defaultdict, OrderedDict, deque, namedtuple, and heapq. These data structures can be useful in specific scenarios and can help you write more efficient and cleaner code.
2. **Decorators**: Decorators in Python are a powerful feature that allows you to modify the behavior of functions or classes without changing their code. They provide a way to "wrap" a function or method with additional functionality, such as logging, memoization, or access control.
3. **Generators and coroutines**: Generators are a type of iterator that allows you to create lazy sequences of values on-the-fly using the **yield** keyword. Coroutines, on the other hand, are a more advanced form of generator that can be used to implement cooperative multitasking and asynchronous programming.
4. **Context managers and the with statement**: Context managers are a convenient way to manage resources such as file handles, sockets, or database connections. They ensure that resources are properly acquired and released, which can help prevent resource leaks and simplify error handling.
5. **Metaclasses and dynamic code generation**: Metaclasses are a powerful, advanced feature that allows you to control the creation of classes in Python. They can be used for various purposes, such as enforcing coding standards, generating code at runtime, or implementing design patterns such as singletons.
6. **Multithreading and multiprocessing**: Python provides various ways to implement concurrent and parallel programming, which can help you take advantage of multi-core processors and improve the performance of your applications.
7. **Networking and web development**: Python has a rich ecosystem of libraries and frameworks for building web applications, working with RESTful APIs, and networking tasks like sockets, HTTP, and more.
8. **Data analysis and machine learning**: Python is a popular language for data analysis, machine learning, and scientific computing. Libraries such as NumPy, pandas, scikit-learn, and TensorFlow make it easy to analyze and manipulate large datasets, perform complex mathematical operations, and train machine learning models.

In order to further expand your knowledge of Python and continue developing your skills as a programmer, we highly recommend that you explore our website: books.cuantum.tech. Here, you will have access to a wide range of highly useful and informative books on Python, as well as other programming languages that you may be interested in.

By delving deeper into the world of programming through our resources, you will be able to gain a deeper understanding of the intricacies of Python and other languages, allowing you to develop more complex and sophisticated programs with greater ease and efficiency. So why wait? Visit our website today and take the next step in your programming journey!

12.2: Popular Python Libraries

Python is a programming language that has gained immense popularity in recent years. One of the reasons for its popularity is its extensive ecosystem of libraries and packages. These libraries are a set of pre-written codes that developers can use in their projects to carry out specific tasks. Python developers can save a lot of time and effort by using these libraries, as they provide ready-to-use solutions for various tasks and problems. In this section, we will briefly introduce some popular Python libraries that you may find useful in your projects.

1. **NumPy (Numerical Python)**: NumPy is the fundamental library for numerical computing in Python. It provides support for working with large, multi-dimensional arrays and matrices, along with a collection of mathematical functions to operate on these arrays.
2. **pandas**: pandas is a powerful library for data manipulation and analysis. It provides data structures like Series and DataFrame, which are designed to handle and manipulate large datasets efficiently. pandas is particularly useful for tasks such as data cleaning, aggregation, and transformation.
3. **matplotlib**: matplotlib is a widely-used library for creating static, animated, and interactive visualizations in Python. It provides a high-level interface for drawing attractive and informative statistical graphics, as well as a low-level interface for customizing the appearance of plots.
4. **seaborn**: seaborn is a data visualization library built on top of matplotlib. It provides a high-level interface for creating informative and attractive statistical graphics, with a focus on visualizing complex datasets using concise and clear syntax.
5. **scikit-learn**: scikit-learn is a popular machine learning library that provides simple and efficient tools for data mining and data analysis. It features various classification, regression, clustering, and dimensionality reduction algorithms, as well as utilities for model selection, evaluation, and preprocessing.
6. **TensorFlow and PyTorch**: TensorFlow and PyTorch are two popular libraries for machine learning and deep learning. Both libraries provide a flexible and efficient platform for building and training neural networks, with support for GPU acceleration and various advanced features.
7. **Flask and Django**: Flask and Django are popular web development frameworks for building web applications in Python. Flask is a lightweight, easy-to-learn framework, while Django is a more comprehensive, full-featured framework that includes a built-in ORM, admin interface, and more.

8. **requests**: requests is a popular library for making HTTP requests in Python. It provides a simple, user-friendly API for sending and receiving data over the internet, making it easy to work with RESTful APIs and web services.
9. **Beautiful Soup and lxml**: Beautiful Soup and lxml are libraries for parsing and navigating HTML and XML documents. They are particularly useful for web scraping, allowing you to extract information from websites and process it programmatically.
10. **SQLAlchemy**: SQLAlchemy is a powerful and flexible Object Relational Mapper (ORM) for Python. It provides a full suite of well-known enterprise-level persistence patterns, designed for efficient and high-performing database access.

These libraries are just a few examples of the vast Python ecosystem, which is constantly growing and evolving. As you continue your Python journey, you'll likely encounter many more libraries that cater to your specific needs and interests.

For instance, if you're interested in web development, you might want to check out Flask or Django, two popular web frameworks. Or if you're working with data, you might find NumPy, Pandas, or SciPy to be useful tools. Always explore the available libraries before implementing a solution from scratch, as it can save you a significant amount of time and effort. By doing so, you can take advantage of the collective knowledge and expertise of the Python community and build more robust and efficient programs.

12.3: Python in Web Development, Data Science, and More

Python's versatility and simplicity make it a popular choice for a variety of domains. In this section, we will briefly explore some of the key areas where Python excels, such as web development, data science, automation, and more.

Web Development:

Python is widely used in web development, thanks to its readability, ease of use, and powerful libraries. Flask and Django are two popular web frameworks that allow developers to build web applications quickly and efficiently. Flask is lightweight and ideal for small to medium-sized projects, while Django is a full-featured framework suitable for larger applications. Both frameworks are well-documented and have extensive community support.

Data Science:

Python has become the go-to language for data science, thanks to its extensive ecosystem of libraries and packages designed for data manipulation, analysis, and visualization. NumPy and pandas provide efficient data structures and operations, while matplotlib and seaborn enable the creation of visualizations to explore and present data. For machine learning and deep learning, scikit-learn, TensorFlow, and PyTorch are popular choices, offering a wide range of tools and algorithms for model building, training, and evaluation.

Automation and Scripting:

Python's simplicity and extensive standard library make it an excellent choice for automation and scripting tasks. You can use Python to automate repetitive tasks, interact with APIs, manipulate files and directories, and much more. Python's cross-platform compatibility also makes it easy to run scripts on different operating systems, such as Windows, macOS, and Linux.

Networking and Security:

Python is a popular language for networking and security professionals, thanks to its powerful libraries and easy-to-read syntax. Libraries such as Scapy, Nmap, and Paramiko allow developers to create network tools, automate security testing, and build custom security applications.

Game Development:

While not as popular as languages like C++ for game development, Python is still used in this domain, particularly for prototyping and building small to medium-sized games. Pygame is a popular library that provides a framework for game development, allowing developers to create 2D games with ease.

Desktop Application Development:

Python can be used to develop cross-platform desktop applications using libraries such as Tkinter, PyQt, or Kivy. These libraries provide graphical user interface (GUI) components that enable developers to create interactive and visually appealing applications that run on various operating systems.

Internet of Things (IoT):

Python is also suitable for IoT development due to its readability, ease of use, and support for various platforms. With libraries like Raspberry Pi GPIO and MicroPython, developers can build and control IoT devices, collect sensor data, and interact with other connected devices.

Conclusion

Python is an incredibly versatile programming language that can be used across a wide range of industries and applications. Its popularity continues to grow, making it an excellent choice for both beginners and seasoned programmers alike.

One of the key advantages of Python is its simplicity, which makes it easy to learn and use. Additionally, Python has a vast ecosystem of libraries, frameworks, and tools that can be leveraged to build complex applications quickly and efficiently. This, coupled with its adaptability, makes Python a go-to choice for developers in various fields.

As you continue your Python journey, you'll find that there are countless areas where Python shines. Whether you're interested in data science, web development, machine learning, or something else entirely, Python has something to offer. By exploring the different domains, you'll be able to identify the ones that are most interesting to you and leverage Python's versatility to tackle projects in those areas. With Python, the possibilities are endless.

12.4: Online Resources and Communities

As you continue your journey with Python, it's essential to be aware of the vast array of online resources and communities that can help you learn, troubleshoot, and collaborate with other developers. In this section, we'll introduce you to some popular resources and communities that will be invaluable as you progress in your Python career.

Cuantum Books

At Quantum Technologies, we take great pride in our team of expert programmers who are constantly pushing the boundaries of what is possible through coding. Our company is founded on the belief that a strong community of programmers is crucial to the success of any project, which is why we have made it our mission to foster an environment of creativity and collaboration.

To help achieve this mission, we have produced a wide range of books designed to guide both beginners and experts alike as they navigate the intricacies of various programming languages and libraries. Our books cover everything from the basics of HTML and CSS to the more complex workings of frameworks like Django and Three.js.

In addition to our books, we also offer a wide range of services for programmers looking to grow their skills. Whether you're looking to learn JavaScript, PHP, Python, or any other programming language, our team of expert instructors can provide you with the guidance and support you need to take your skills to the next level.

So why not join us on your journey to become a master programmer? Visit books.quantum.tech today to see our full range of books and services and start taking your skills to the next level!

Official Python Documentation:

The official Python documentation (https://docs.python.org/) is an excellent starting point for understanding Python's core language features and standard library. It provides comprehensive and up-to-date information about Python syntax, built-in functions, modules, and more. The documentation is available for multiple Python versions and can be downloaded for offline use.

Python Package Index (PyPI):

PyPI (https://pypi.org/) is the official repository for Python packages. You can search for, download, and install packages created by the Python community using the 'pip' tool. PyPI contains packages for a wide range of applications, from web development to data analysis, and more.

Stack Overflow:

Stack Overflow (https://stackoverflow.com/) is an invaluable resource for developers of all skill levels. It's a question and answer platform where you can search for answers to your Python-related questions or post your own queries. Chances are, someone has already encountered a similar issue, and you can benefit from their experience and the community's collective knowledge.

GitHub:

GitHub (https://github.com/) is a platform for version control and collaboration that hosts millions of open-source projects, many of which are Python-based. You can search for projects, learn from their code, contribute to them, or even create your own repositories to showcase your work and collaborate with others.

Real Python:

Real Python (https://realpython.com/) is a comprehensive learning platform that offers tutorials, articles, and courses on various Python topics. They cover beginner to advanced subjects, including web development, data science, and more. The platform provides practical examples and clear explanations, making it a valuable resource for Python learners.

Python.org **Community:**

The official Python website (https://www.python.org/community/) offers numerous resources, including mailing lists, discussion forums, and a list of Python User Groups (PUGs) worldwide. Joining a local PUG is a great way to network with other Python enthusiasts, learn from their experiences, and collaborate on projects.

Reddit:

The Python subreddit (https://www.reddit.com/r/Python/) is an active community where you can find news, articles, discussions, and resources related to Python. You can also ask questions, share your projects, and engage with other Python developers.

YouTube:

Many Python developers and educators maintain YouTube channels with tutorials and explanations on various Python topics. Some popular channels include Corey Schafer (https://www.youtube.com/user/schafer5) and Programming with Mosh (https://www.youtube.com/user/programmingwithmosh), among others. These channels offer video tutorials that can help you understand complex concepts through visual explanations.

These are just a few examples of the numerous online resources and communities available to Python developers. As you continue learning and expanding your Python skills, don't hesitate to explore these resources, ask questions, and engage with the community. The Python ecosystem is vast and supportive, and you'll find that fellow developers are often more than happy to help and share their knowledge. Good luck on your Python journey, and happy coding!

Conclusion

Congratulations on completing this book! You have gained a comprehensive understanding of Python topics, from fundamental language concepts to advanced topics such as object-oriented programming and error handling. Not only have you learned about best practices, but you have also worked on a project and discovered resources to help you continue your Python journey.

As you continue to explore and develop your skills as a Python developer, it is important to remember that programming is a continuous learning process. The Python ecosystem is vast, and there are numerous libraries, tools, and applications across various fields. With the foundation you have built through this book, you are now well-equipped to dive deeper into your areas of interest, such as web development, data science, automation, or any other field where Python is applicable.

Remember that the Python community is supportive and always willing to assist. Take advantage of online resources, engage with other members of the community, and do not hesitate to ask questions. As you gain more experience, consider giving back by assisting others, contributing to open-source projects, or sharing your knowledge through articles, tutorials, or talks.

Lastly, strive to continuously improve yourself. Keep learning, stay curious, and embrace challenges as opportunities for growth. As you progress on your Python journey, you will discover that the skills you have acquired can open doors to new and exciting opportunities and can help you make a significant impact in your chosen field.

We appreciate you selecting this book as a stepping stone in your Python journey, and we wish you the very best in your future endeavors as you continue to explore the captivating world of Python programming. Happy coding!

Where to continue?

If you've completed this book, and are hungry for more programming knowledge, we'd like to recommend some other books from our software company that you might find useful. These books cover a wide range of topics and are designed to help you continue to expand your programming skills.

1. "Master Web Development with Django" - This book is a comprehensive guide to building web applications using Django, one of the most popular Python web frameworks. It covers everything from setting up your development environment to deploying your application to a production server.
2. "Mastering React" - React is a popular JavaScript library for building user interfaces. This book will help you master the core concepts of React and show you how to build powerful, dynamic web applications.
3. "Data Analysis with Python" - Python is a powerful language for data analysis, and this book will help you unlock its full potential. It covers topics such as data cleaning, data manipulation, and data visualization, and provides you with practical exercises to help you apply what you've learned.
4. "Machine Learning with Python" - Machine learning is one of the most exciting fields in computer science, and this book will help you get started with building your own machine learning models using Python. It covers topics such as linear regression, logistic regression, and decision trees.
5. "Natural Language Processing with Python" - Natural language processing is a field that focuses on the interaction between computers and humans using natural language. This book will help you get started with building your own natural language processing applications using Python. It covers topics such as text preprocessing, sentiment analysis, and text classification.

All of these books are designed to help you continue to expand your programming skills and deepen your understanding of the Python language. We believe that programming is a skill that can be learned and developed over time, and we are committed to providing resources to help you achieve your goals.

We'd also like to take this opportunity to thank you for choosing our software company as your guide in your programming journey. We hope that you have found this book of Python for beginners to be a valuable resource, and we look forward to continuing to provide you with high-quality programming resources in the future. If you have any feedback or suggestions for future books or resources, please don't hesitate to get in touch with us. We'd love to hear from you!

See you soon!

As we reach the end of this comprehensive guide to Python programming, it's time to reflect on the journey we've taken together. Over the course of this book, we've delved into various aspects of Python, building a strong foundation in programming concepts and best practices, while also giving you the tools and knowledge to tackle real-world projects.

In Chapter 1, we began by introducing you to the world of Python and its history. You learned about Python's creator, Guido van Rossum, the Zen of Python, and the reasons behind Python's widespread popularity. We also discussed Python's applications in various domains, such as web development, data analysis, and artificial intelligence.

Chapter 2 focused on setting up your Python environment. We walked you through the installation process, and you learned about Integrated Development Environments (IDEs) and their benefits. We also introduced you to Jupyter Notebook, a powerful tool for interactive programming, especially in the field of data science.

In Chapter 3, we dove into Python's basic syntax and data types. We covered variables, strings, numbers, lists, tuples, sets, and dictionaries. You also learned about various operations that you can perform on these data types, providing you with a solid foundation to write more complex programs.

Chapter 4 explored control flow and loops. We discussed if-else statements, for loops, and while loops, which are essential for controlling the flow of your programs. You practiced writing more advanced code, incorporating logic and iteration, enabling you to solve more complex problems.

In Chapter 5, we introduced you to functions, a crucial aspect of programming that promotes code reusability and modularity. We discussed the importance of functions, how to define them, and how to use them effectively in your programs. We also covered Python's built-in functions and lambda functions.

Chapter 6 delved into file handling, which is essential for working with data stored in files. You learned how to read from and write to files, manipulate file paths, and work with various file formats such as CSV and JSON.

In Chapter 7, we explored Python modules and packages. We discussed the concept of modules, their benefits, and how to create and import them. We also covered Python packages, how to create and use them, and how to install external packages using pip.

Chapter 8 introduced you to the world of object-oriented programming (OOP). We discussed the fundamental concepts of OOP, such as classes, objects, inheritance, polymorphism, and encapsulation. You learned how to create classes, define methods, and work with inheritance to model real-world scenarios.

In Chapter 9, we tackled error handling and exceptions. We covered common Python errors, how to handle exceptions using try-except blocks, raising exceptions, and creating custom exceptions. This knowledge is vital for building robust and resilient applications.

Chapter 10 focused on Python best practices. We discussed the PEP 8 style guide, code commenting and documentation, naming conventions, and the importance of code reusability and modularization. By following these best practices, you can write clean, maintainable, and efficient code that is easier for others to understand and work with.

In Chapter 11, we guided you through the process of building a simple application from scratch. We covered project planning, implementation, testing, debugging, deployment, and distribution. By working on the TaskMaster project, you applied the concepts and skills you learned throughout the book, reinforcing your understanding and gaining valuable hands-on experience.

Finally, in Chapter 12, we looked at the next steps in your Python journey. We introduced you to advanced Python topics, popular Python libraries, and the diverse applications of Python in various fields. We also provided you with a list of online resources and communities to help you continue learning and growing as a Python programmer.

To summarize, this book has given you a comprehensive understanding of Python programming, from the basics to more advanced topics. You've explored Python's rich ecosystem, learned best practices, and applied your knowledge to build a real-world application. We hope that this journey has been enjoyable, informative, and inspiring, and that you now feel confident in your ability to tackle a wide range of Python projects.

As you continue your Python journey, remember that learning is an ongoing process. The world of programming is constantly evolving, and there is always more to discover. Stay curious, keep exploring, and don't be afraid to ask questions or seek help from the vibrant Python community. Engage with others, share your experiences, and learn from the collective wisdom of fellow programmers.

Moreover, as you gain experience, consider giving back to the community by contributing to open-source projects, mentoring beginners, or sharing your knowledge through blog posts, tutorials, or presentations. By doing so, you not only help others grow but also reinforce your own understanding and gain valuable experience.

In closing, we'd like to thank you for embarking on this Python journey with us. We hope that the knowledge and skills you've gained will empower you to create innovative solutions, advance your career, and make a meaningful impact on the world. Keep learning, keep growing, and enjoy the exciting adventure that lies ahead.

Happy coding!

Know more about us

At Cuantum Technologies, we specialize in building web applications that deliver creative experiences and solve real-world problems. Our developers have expertise in a wide range of programming languages and frameworks, including Python, Django, React, Three.js, and Vue.js, among others. We are constantly exploring new technologies and techniques to stay at the forefront of the industry, and we pride ourselves on our ability to create solutions that meet our clients' needs.

If you are interested in learning more about our Cuantum Technologies and the services that we offer, please visit our website at books.cuantum.tech. We would be happy to answer any questions that you may have and to discuss how we can help you with your software development needs.

CUANTUM
TECHNOLOGIES

www.cuantum.tech

Made in United States
North Haven, CT
05 September 2023